W9-AHO-165

THERE'S NO SUCH THING AS A BAD KID

THERE'S NO SUCH THING AS A BAD KID

TITUS O'NEIL
WITH PAUL GUZZO

Published by ECW Press
665 Gerrard Street East
Toronto, Ontario, Canada M4M 1Y2
416-694-3348 / info@ecwpress.com

Editor for the Press: Michael Holmes
Cover design: Rodney Githens and
Adam McGinnis
Cover photo © Craig Ambrosio / WWE
Cover image © WWE

PRINTED AND BOUND IN CANADA

To the best of his abilities, the author has related
experiences, places, people, and organizations
from his memories of them. In order to protect
the privacy of others, he has, in some instances,
changed the names of certain people and details of
events and places.

The statements and opinions expressed in this work
are solely those of the author and do not reflect
the views of WWE. WWE hereby disclaims any
responsibility for such statements and opinions,
and they should not be construed as representing
WWE's position on any subject.

LIBRARY AND ARCHIVES CANADA CATALOGUING
IN PUBLICATION

Title: There's no such thing as a bad kid : how I
went from stereotype to prototype / Titus O'Neil
with Paul Guzzo.

Names: O'Neil, Titus, author. | Guzzo, Paul, author.

Identifiers: Canadiana (print) 20190110052X
Canadiana (ebook) 20190110589

ISBN 978-1-77041-492-1 (hardcover)
ISBN 978-1-77305-425-4 (PDF)
ISBN 978-1-77305-424-7 (ePUB)

Subjects: LCSH: O'Neil, Titus. | LCSH: O'Neil,
Titus—Childhood and youth. | LCSH: Wrestlers—
United States—Biography.

Classification: LCC GV1196.O54 A3 2019 |
DDC 796.812092—dc23

PRINTING: FRIESENS   5   4   3   2   1

MIX
Paper from
responsible sources
FSC® C016245

I dedicate this book to my amazing mother, Daria Bullard, who provided a foundation of caring, consideration, compassion, loyalty and love to me, my brothers, Ted, Corey and Clifford, and all who came in contact with our family. Also included in this dedication are the great men and women who supported and served thousands of kids through the Florida Sheriffs Youth Ranches that gave me, along with many others, a place to turn our troubles into triumphs.

To Charles Blalock, Pastor Greg Powe, all of my Bullard Family Foundation board, staff, volunteers, partners and supporters: thank you. I would not have achieved this degree of success in changing the lives of thousands of families without your guidance and help.

And last, but certainly not least: to my amazing two sons, Thaddeus (TJ) and Titus Bullard. I'm so proud to have the honor of being your father. I love and appreciate the men you are and the powerful, positive and loving forces that you continue to be in this world. Always live by our family's top three rules and I'll never be disappointed in you:

1. Love and respect everyone you come in contact with. (You may not like some of them and their ways, but love and respect them.)
2. Don't use the word "can't." We *can* do all things through Christ.
3. Be *your* best! You will struggle and fail at some things in life, but as long as you know that you gave your best effort, you will not disappoint yourself, God, or anyone else.

With love, honor and gratitude,
Thaddeus Bullard
aka WWE Superstar "Titus O'Neil"

CHAPTER 1

There is no such thing as a bad kid.

Too often in our society, children are labeled based on their behavior, economic status, religion, or race. The stereotypes that go along with these labels can have a devastating effect. These kids can carry this stigma with them through adulthood, and they may even begin to believe that the stereotype is who they really are.

Let's talk about the stigmas and stereotypes that go hand in hand with the phrase "bad kid." When kids misbehave in class, teachers, caregivers, and parents can be quick to dismiss labels more properly belonging to diagnoses of medical, emotional, or behavioral conditions. Instead, they reduce those children to two dreaded words: "bad kid." The purpose of this book is to not only shed some light on many of the issues facing our children but also reveal why we must learn to act and talk in a manner that consciously eradicates the phrase. "Bad kid" should never be uttered again to describe a child.

I didn't write this book as a philosopher or a theologian. I wrote this book because I was once labeled a bad kid. Had it not been for the people in my life who supported me, and one man in particular who told 12-year-old me that "there is no such thing as a bad kid," the words that you are about to read would be completely different — if ever written at all.

This is not just the story of my past. It is also a tale I continue to share with youth around the world, with the hope of positively affecting both the present and future.

I want adults who were once labeled bad kids but had someone pushing them in the right direction, helping to get them out of a bad situation and providing them with much needed counseling, to relate to the stories in this book. We all have a duty to help those so-called bad kids when we encounter them, whether they are mirror images of ourselves or not. But I also want this book to be a revelation for those whose childhoods went smoothly. Do not judge a man, woman, or child whose shoes you have never walked in; instead, understand that the circumstances of someone's life can affect who that person becomes.

I was once wrongly judged and labeled because no one took the time to understand my circumstances ...

In the summer of 1976, Daria Bullard was raped in her St. Augustine, Florida, home.

She was 11 years old.

Her attacker was someone she knew.

She gave birth to a son in Boynton Beach's Bethesda Memorial Hospital on April 29, 1977.

You know me as WWE Superstar Titus O'Neil, but that's just a character I play on TV. My real name is Thaddeus Bullard. Daria is my mom, and I am the product of that rape.

Though I obviously have no recollection of the hospital room in which I was born, I am willing to bet it was the nicest place I stayed as a young child. My mom was a kid herself; she did her best to raise me, but it was always a financial struggle.

I should have ended up in a much different and worse situation than I am in today. At a young age, I was regularly told that I would end up in prison or dead, and for much of my childhood, I was on a path to prove those people right. I fought too much. I screwed around too much. I yelled at adults too much. I didn't study enough. I was labeled a bad kid by too many people to count. I was living up to those low expectations.

Yet, as I write these words, I know that I am a good man and a success — and neither has anything to do with my status as a WWE Superstar. Being a WWE Superstar is what I do for a living, but it is not who I *am* for a living.

I am a man who played football for and then graduated from the University of Florida. I am a man who went from troubled kid from the projects to elected vice president of that university's student body. I am a man who every year makes sure that thousands of the Tampa Bay area's underprivileged kids wake up to presents under their Christmas tree and receive backpacks, lunch boxes, and classroom supplies before the school year. I am a man who relishes my job as a father and role model to two sons.

I am a man who proves that how you are labeled as a child does not have to define who you will become as an adult. I am a man who lives every day as proof that there is no such thing as a bad kid.

I want to spread that message to every corner of the globe. I am not a psychiatrist or psychologist, but I believe, with every fiber of my being, that we cannot shallowly state that a kid is bad and think that is that; I want adults to understand that we need to look deeper than a child's behavior. While it's possible their financial situation may play a role in their actions, we need to look past that. Kids from rich, poor, and middle-class families can all share common problems. We have to look at their family life. We have to look at the educational barriers they may face. Maybe the child is getting bullied at school. Maybe the child has an undiagnosed learning disability. Maybe the child is physically or verbally abused at home. We have to take those issues and others into account. In doing so, we can transform the lives of countless children.

No child is inherently bad — it is only until we understand why the child is misbehaving that we can help to remedy the situation. And if you are not personally equipped to help, find someone who is.

If someone was struck by a car in a hit-and-run accident in front of your house, would you look at that person and say, "I'd like to help, but I'm not a doctor . . . " and then walk away? Or would you call 911?

I might not be an expert in the field, but my life experience has given me a unique perspective. It is from that experience that I believe the following: Ignoring a child in need may suppress their hope for a better future. Helping to transform that child may open their eyes not only to hope but to a whole new world of possibility. For much of my childhood, I was called a bad kid — period. Had no one stepped in to examine why I acted the way I did, perhaps I would have proven my naysayers correct and ended up dead or in jail. When I finally met people willing to see the big picture surrounding my issues, they realized I did not come from my mother's womb cursing and fighting. They understood I was reacting to my environment. They sought to understand the causes of my behavior and then realized I could be saved through a positive, structured, and disciplined environment. That was what gave me hope.

I owe those individuals everything and have since dedicated my life to paying their faith forward.

My beginning was not very good, but there was nothing I could do about that.

I can, however, dictate my ending, and it will be special.

CHAPTER 2

*L*et's eat.
　　Hungry.
Where's the food?

If you follow me on social media —
@TitusONeilWWE — you know that when I am
traveling, whether it is with WWE or for personal reasons, I post one of those three phrases the
moment my plane lands. And, within a few hours,
I'll post a photo of a plate of food that is as much a
work of art as it is a meal.

I'm a foodie. I have been for at least 20 years.

One of the best parts of my lifestyle is that it
allows me to fully indulge that foodie-ness.

When I'm in New York, I look for great cheese-
cake and pizza. In the South, I want to eat at great

farm-to-table restaurants. On the West Coast, all I want is fantastic sushi. In Germany, I'll crave the best schnitzel. In places like Japan, South Africa, and South America, I'll look for a good steak. But I am not just some big greedy individual running around, stuffing his face. What I appreciate most is the fact that I have options — as a kid I didn't have any.

There aren't many types of foods I don't like either. In my travels, I always make an effort to try foods I never thought I'd have access to — eel, alligator, bison, the list goes on and on. There is nothing I will not taste at least once.

That said, there are some foods I absolutely refuse to eat today, like egg noodles and frozen bags of mixed sweet peas and carrots. It's not so much the taste; rather, they conjure up negative memories of my childhood.

Food can be about more than the things we put in our mouths. Food can be a definition of who we are, where we come from, and what we must overcome.

When I look back on my childhood, all the food I was served was inexpensive and very unhealthy: neck bones, hot dogs, fried pork chops, smothered pork chops and chicken, Spam, bologna, pork and beans, government cheese that came in hard square blocks, government peanut butter that could bend a knife, and an assortment of dessert and breakfast options made with Jiffy muffin mixes.

And those egg noodles and frozen peas and carrots

were included at just about every dinner. It is why they remind me of the struggles of my childhood. If someone had told me that I'd one day be dining at five-star restaurants on the regular, I'd look at them like they were crazy. As a kid, I ate what my mom put forward, no matter what it was; it was fuel for our bodies. We didn't have much, but we made do with what we had.

When my grandmother learned my mom was pregnant, she took her to Boynton Beach for an abortion. My mom had second thoughts and refused. Furious with that decision, my grandmother threw my mom out of the house. My mom, who was 12 when I was born, was taken in by her friend Cherlene's grandparents in Delray Beach. Those nice folks looked after me during the day so that my mom could continue her education.

But by the time I was three, my mom — still a kid, remember — had started getting into trouble at school and lashing out at adults, including Cherlene's grandparents. She voluntarily placed me in foster care while she was counseled for anger that stemmed from the rape that she hid from just about everyone, including me, for many years.

Not long after, my mom began dating her friend's cousin, Clifford, and within a few months was pregnant with his child. My mom dropped out of school, took me back, and, along with Clifford, we moved into a two-bedroom apartment on Fifth Avenue in

Delray Beach. Locals nicknamed our neighborhood "The Hole" because it was a dead-end street: there was only one way in and one way out. And, like a big hole, the neighborhood seemed impossible to escape. The only reason to ever be in The Hole was because you were stuck living there or were buying drugs or stolen goods.

It was there, on my fourth birthday, that my brother Clifford Jr. was born. A lot of kids may have a problem with sharing a birthday with a sibling; it usually means sharing the spotlight at your parties. But we never had that issue — we never had birthday parties. We weren't even guaranteed presents. And some years, instead of a cake, we each received a single cupcake made from Jiffy mix.

The only birthday parties I experienced as a child were those I attended, oftentimes without a present for the birthday kid. The parties were typically the same — hot dogs and hamburgers, tater tots, those small bags of chips, cake, and red-and-blue Bomb Pops. For me, those foods will be forever synonymous with kids' parties. Sometimes at WWE, when catering includes hot dogs and tater tots, I'll yell, "Whose birthday party is it?"

When I was a child, my mom was clear: she could not afford to throw me a birthday party. So I never expected one.

Santa Claus? She never let me believe in him. If I received a present, it was because she worked hard.

We believed in God and His blessings, not some magical man who flew on reindeer and snuck into homes. Plus, if other kids received 10 toys from Santa and I received only one, I'd have thought I had done something wrong.

The only holiday we went all out to celebrate was Thanksgiving, because we would be invited to a relative's home, typically one of my aunts'. The adults would play dominoes and cards in the front room, while the cousins — 15 of us — would play football and basketball outside. Come dinnertime, everyone ate like it was our last meal.

When I was six, money got even tighter. On January 30, 1984, my brother Corey was born. Then, just 11 months later, on December 28, 1984, my mom gave birth to my brother Ted.

I have always gotten along with my siblings and have never thought of them as half-brothers. Unfortunately, I never respected their dad, Clifford. In my opinion, he did not exude a positive image of what a parent should be, and I never looked at him as a father figure.

Every child needs positive parental figures, mentors, and role models at home. I feel like a lot of the problems we have in our society are because of a lack of this positive influence.

Role models can vary. They can be a single mother or father, both a mom and a dad, or two moms, or two dads. Every family is different, but the one commonality should be that there is a strong parental presence to shape the minds, hearts, and principles of a child.

My mom, a single mom, was a great role model, even if I didn't realize it at the time. She led by example through her strength and determination to provide for us.

Still, for whatever reason, I also needed a positive father figure. Every child is different. Many children grow into fine adults without ever having a traditional father or mother figure in their life. Many moms fill that fatherly void, and vice versa. Many children embrace their mothers in dual roles as fathers. My mom was strong enough to be a father as well. But I just couldn't see that at the time.

The closest thing I had to a positive father figure in my childhood was Charles. Charles was my mom's ex-boyfriend, from before she met Clifford. Charles had agreed to pretend he was my father to hide how I was really conceived.

He'd come around every so often and bring me small presents and play with me. But even as a naive little kid, I never believed he was my dad. There was no emotional connection. When I was seven or eight, his visits became less frequent. Eventually, my "father," Charles, was never mentioned again. I didn't think much of it; like me, so many of my friends didn't have fathers either.

All I had was Clifford.

He drank too much. He didn't seem to have a great work ethic. He never showed my mom the respect she deserved as a mother of four who worked hard as a waitress and as a parent. Did I respect my mother as I much as I should have? No — but I was a kid. He was a grown man who was supposed to teach me to respect women.

I never wanted to be Clifford's son, and, in my opinion, he never tried to be a dad to me. He was just some dude in the house. Arguments were the norm, and I'd let him know how I felt, and he'd let me know he didn't care. But when he was drunk, he could get abusive, in my view, and sometimes the arguments would escalate to violence. I never hit him back, but I sure as hell wanted to.

I never want to be compared to Clifford, so as an adult, I work hard to avoid many of his negative behaviors. For example, while I'll have an occasional glass of red wine, I've made it a point to never get drunk. You'll never see me drinking a six-pack of beer or taking shots with my friends. I've been drunk only once in my life. I was a sophomore in college, and it was so bad that Cara Evans, one of my best friends, had to help me home, shower me, get me in bed, and make sure I didn't choke on my own vomit. The next day, I felt terrible.

My mom felt stuck. If our family was barely making it with two incomes, what would happen with one?

She got her answer a little less than two years after my youngest brother was born. Clifford left her. My mom, a 21-year-old without a high school education, was suddenly left to raise four boys on her own. A year later, we moved to the Boynton Terrace Apartments, Section 8 housing — the projects.

Our apartment wasn't too bad. We had three bedrooms — I split a room with my brother Clifford — and two bathrooms, so the wait to shower was never too long. We also had a small television, though the kids rarely had a say in what was on; that was up to my mother. She loved *Dallas*, which I hated until I ultimately got swept up in the soap opera plots. *MacGyver* was another one of her favorites.

What I liked most were shows like *Good Times* and *Sanford and Son* because I related to the characters and stories. Those shows were groundbreaking and opened America's eyes to what truly goes on in the African American community. They were sitcoms, but they also tackled serious issues — such as homelessness and racism — both overtly and covertly. Maybe the characters were a little too stereotypical at times, but for the most part, those programs truly represented the reality of Black America and our culture. Plus, it was just fun to see characters who looked, talked, and lived like me.

But if there was a television program that best summarized the Boynton Beach projects, it is *Miami*

Vice — and I'm not talking about the glamorous scenes with the fancy cars and parties.

I grew up in South Florida in the 1980s, at the height of the crack epidemic. That drug was my neighborhood's economic driver and destroyer. It was sold everywhere — on corners, in apartments, from cars. Occasionally, we'd witness what we called a "jump out" — when an undercover cop would jump from an unmarked car to make a sudden arrest. Still, the police presence was not as strong as it should have been. If law enforcement had wanted, they could have found crimes committed in my neighborhood 24 hours a day.

Among the neighborhood drug dealers was the father of one of my friends.

I will make this perfectly clear: I do not condone selling drugs or illegal substances to anyone. I am very discouraged by the lifestyle in which my friend's father chose to get caught up.

Still, I will not blanket judge him.

I do believe, at one point, there was plenty of good in him. I do not know what led him to that lifestyle. But I do know that being in that lifestyle did not automatically make him a bad person.

Again, I do not believe there is such thing as bad people. I think people make bad decisions, and they are hardened by life.

In my opinion, a big hit to the working class from an economic standpoint came in the 1980s. In the

1970s and early 1980s, men and women with little or no education could earn good money working in factories. Those jobs also provided great pensions, benefits, and everything else needed to help those employees realize the American dream. And then in the mid-1980s, across the country, those factory employment opportunities disappeared for a mix of reasons, including automation and globalization. Those working-class people had to find other careers. Unfortunately, some of those individuals turned to selling drugs.

I don't know if my friend's father started dealing because he couldn't find other high-paying work — and I'll never know. But I'll never judge a man until I know his whole story; there is always more to every scenario than what we see on the surface. I could never view him as simply being a bad person. I just knew that he made a bad decision with the lifestyle he chose.

Looking back, I believe my friend's father also disapproved of his line of work, so he sought to remedy that in other ways. He had high hopes for his son, always reminding him not to follow in his footsteps and to not sell drugs. He was an altruistic man too. He paid for my cleats for my first season of Pop Warner football. He helped single mothers who didn't have enough money to buy school supplies. When he threw barbecues, his son's friends were invited.

It was at one of those barbecues that I saw him get murdered.

I was 11 years old, the grown-ups were on the porch playing cards and dominoes as usual. The kids, about 10 of us that day, were doing what we usually did too — playing a game we called throw 'em up, blow 'em up. The rules were simple: one kid tossed the ball up into the air, and whoever caught it then tried to run for a touchdown without getting blown up by the rest of the kids. As we played, an off-white Impala — probably a 1979 or 1980 model — drove past us and stopped in front of my friend's home. The car windows rolled down, and someone shot my friend's dad, first in the leg and then, as he turned to run, in his back. When he fell, they shot him one more time in the chest, and they drove away.

My friend's aunt frantically yelled for someone to call 911. I was frozen in fear until another adult ushered me into a nearby home.

My friend sat next to his dad and watched him die.

I am not a helicopter parent. Still, because that moment haunts me, I am overprotective when it comes to keeping my sons away from any kind of criminal activity. I never want them to witness what I saw, nor do I ever want them to be so close to having their lives cut short because of the poor decisions of a person who is standing nearby.

My friend later turned to drug dealing and has spent most of his adult life in and out of prison.

Would he have turned out differently had his dad not been killed and been around to continually remind his son to strive for something better than a life of crime? Perhaps. Would my friend have not felt the need to sell drugs if his father had been there to pay the bills? Perhaps.

I don't know what decision he would've made had his dad not been murdered. I know where my route took me, where his route took him, and what we both became. But because I don't know what it's like to walk in his shoes, I will never judge him. I am certain that under different circumstances he could have had a much different life.

Drugs were impossible to avoid in my neighborhood. When my mom had to work the night or weekend shift, I was at times left in the care of drug users, sometimes neighbors and sometimes family. Don't judge my mom based on your life experiences. She had nowhere else to send me — babysitters were not in the budget, and leaving me home alone in my neighborhood was actually a less safe option.

At a young age, I could tell when someone was high. It was more than just the red eyes. They were paranoid and antsy. They looked much older than they were. The worst addicts had rotting teeth.

In the projects, I'd see crack being smoked in public outside, but those looking after me tried to hide it. They'd light up in a bathroom or a bedroom. Sometimes, they'd forget to lock the bathroom door, and I'd walk in on them smoking. Pushing their foot against the door, they'd yell for me to come back later as though they could keep their doings a secret. I knew what was going on even when I didn't see them puffing on a pipe — the pungent aroma would take over the entire apartment, or crumpled Budweiser cans poked with pin holes that were used in lieu of crack pipes would be all over the floor.

Most of the kids in my school came from similar situations. I'd estimate well over half of my fellow students were Black, and in Boynton Beach in the '80s, that meant I knew that well over half of my fellow students were poor.

The white kids — I thought they lived the life. I stress that I *thought*. Looking back on my childhood as an adult, I realize my white classmates likely had problems of their own at home. I realize money alone does not make someone happy. I also realize that it's unlikely that every one of my white classmates was rich.

However, because not a single Black kid I knew had ever been on a ritzy vacation, and I did hear white kids talking about luxurious trips, I just thought that was how our town was divided. I thought Black kids were poor and white kids were rich.

Some of my white classmates would talk about spending the weekend at Disney World or going to the beach in Sarasota or Siesta Key, and it blew my mind. Sure, my mom took us to the public beaches near our home once or twice a year, but that was a much difference experience. While it wasn't dirty, it wasn't welcoming either. The white students' weekend or week-long excursions sounded like trips to paradise. But I was never jealous of the white kids; they were white, I rationalized. That's just what white people did.

I was, however, somewhat envious of the Black kids in my neighborhood who might have been poor but still had the financial means to do some things on occasion that I wasn't able to. My family was among the worst off in a neighborhood made up of Boynton Beach's poorest. I'd hear one of my friends say he was going to the movie theater, and I'd think, "Hey, I want to go to the movie theater. Why does this Black kid from the projects have money to go and I don't?"

When I'd see a kid with new shoes, I'd get angry that I had talking shoes that were not name brand. People who were poor understand what a talking shoe is: it's when the sole comes loose and flaps like a mouth when you walk.

When I did get "new" shoes, they weren't actually new. They were often hand-me-downs, given to me by someone who didn't fit into them anymore. They were scuffed and faded and smelled like someone else's feet. Yes, people of all economic backgrounds are raised on hand-me-downs. But in my neighborhood and neighborhoods like mine, hand-me-downs are sometimes not handed down until they are just weeks away from talking. Or they are handed down through multiple families before they reach their final destination, which was oftentimes me.

Much of my wardrobe was also donated to us. I wasn't as big as I am today, but I was tall and lanky. By the time I was 10, I was five-foot-ten, weighed 150 pounds, and wore a size 11 shoe. It was hard enough to find clothes for someone that awkwardly sized, never mind also age appropriate.

For quite a while I needed glasses, but we couldn't afford a pair. I was too embarrassed to let anyone know we were so poor, so I pretended I could see. I would hide in the back of the classroom to avoid being called on to read the blackboard. I could read up close, but the moment the blackboard became the teaching tool, I checked out. Being ill-prepared for tests, I'd just fill in random answer bubbles and hope for the best, but I really didn't care whether or not it worked out in my favor.

My mom's social worker, Barbara Wilfork, helped me to get glasses when I was in the third or fourth grade. But that made my situation worse. Sure, I could learn — but at that age, the glasses made me a target. My sight was real bad. Those glasses didn't look like bifocals; they were more like quad-focals. I looked like the younger brother of Redd Foxx's character in *Harlem Nights*.

So, it should go without saying that as a five-foot-ten lanky kid with talking shoes, geeky clothes, and thick glasses, I was picked on. I'd walk my school hallways and kids would yell, "Four eyes," "Pull your shoes up," or "You could walk across the ocean in those pants and stay dry."

My only regular respite as a young child was my grandmother. She came back into my family's life when I was four.

My mother and grandmother's relationship never fully recovered. Still, my mom found it in her heart to forgive my grandmother, who sometimes looked after me. She'd take me fishing and always bait the hook. Worms grossed me out. Or we'd watch sports — which I loved but were rarely on the television at home — or we'd watch WWE. My favorite wrestler was Junkyard Dog.

I still recall one of Junkyard Dog's matches in Green Bay, Wisconsin. To me, it was surprising and fascinating that the predominantly white crowd unanimously cheered him. I thought, "This dude can go to Green Bay, Wisconsin, and defeat a white opponent, and everyone is cheering for him. He's a hero." Those people were not fixated on color, like I was at the time. They looked at Junkyard Dog as the gifted performer he was and said, "That guy is our dude, and we don't want anyone to mess with him." He was a truly unifying presence. It was through him that I realized that America can be a great place when we want it to be. It was beautiful. And today, that serves as a constant reminder of the positive influence that I can have as a WWE Superstar to bring people of all backgrounds together.

My grandmother, on the other hand, could not be swayed from her favorite: Dusty Rhodes. I can see why. They were very much alike. They were both charismatic underdogs who refused to be kept down.

Have you ever seen the show *Mama's Family*? My grandmother was just like Mama, but Black. She was five-foot-five, but you'd think she was seven feet tall. She was outgoing. She smoked. She drank. She was a fighter. If she didn't like something you said to her, she'd be right in your face, cigarette in one hand, drink in another, shouting you down. That part of her personality definitely rubbed off on me, minus the cigarette and drink.

My grandmother did not need a man to fight her battles. She was single and owned a soul food bar near her home in Delray Beach. Real blue-collar types were regulars. I witnessed her putting those rough, grown men in check on more than one occasion. "Y'all aren't about to act like that around my grandson," she'd yell. I won't lie. I preferred being with my grandmother over being at home with my mother. I hated everything about my life, and I blamed my mom.

We didn't have money for parties. We didn't have money to go out to eat. We didn't have money to go to the movie theater. We didn't have money for Christmas gifts. We didn't have money for school supplies. "Damn," I'd think, "what *do* we have money for?"

She didn't tell me how I was conceived until I was a teenager, and I was too young to realize that my mom was a kid herself. She was my mom, so I looked at her as an adult. I'd wonder why she didn't have a better job that paid more money. I thought she was a failure. I felt she could do better but chose not to. My friends had x, y, and z . . . so why didn't we?

I was disrespectful. If she told me to do something, I'd do the exact opposite. If she told me to sit, I'd stand. If she told me to do my homework, I'd put my books away. Hell, she could have told me to douse our house fire with water, and I would have tossed gasoline onto the flames. I was a terrible son. My mom was filled with her own anger, too, so she didn't really know how to handle me. She'd spank me when I wouldn't back down, which means she spanked me a lot, but she never crossed the line. The same goes for my teachers, principals, and other family members. It was a different culture back then. Each was allowed to smack my butt, and even though no one was excessive, the totality of all that spanking added up. I had an abusive childhood, but I never considered anyone in my life to be abusive.

The spankings were always a result of my wrongdoings, but they always infuriated me. Everyone was quick to discipline me, but no one was willing to ask me why I was acting out. Rather than taming me, the whuppings fueled my rage. Physical punishment doesn't teach children anything; instead, they become immune to it and begin to mimic the violent behavior, just as I did. I believe this not from experience as a father of two sons and mentor to countless other kids, but as a child who was raised in a spanking and yelling environment.

The most epic whupping I ever received was given out by my mom, at my school. I don't know if this is a Black thing or if it was just a thing at my school when I was growing up, but you knew a public licking was coming if a Black mom walked into a school because her son had gotten into trouble.

Those women wouldn't even bother to take the curlers out of their hair or change out of their pajamas if it was early morning. They'd angrily march through those hallways with a switch in their hand and a look on their face that said, "Oh, you want to get in trouble? You want to show your ass at school? I'll come up here and show my ass too." They'd then find a place to whup their son, and then turn and leave, while muttering, "Don't make me come back here."

Admittedly, it was funny to watch a friend get beaten by his mom in public. We'd all start clowning on him once she was out of the building. It wasn't so funny when it happened to me.

At Spadey Elementary School, Principal Kramer believed in corporal punishment, but he was also a reasonable man. Sometimes, after hearing me out, he'd see the situation from my perspective and decide against punishment. But he couldn't let the teachers know that. To make it seem like he sided with the teachers, he would whack his chair cushion with a paddle.

If you screwed up big time — meaning you disrespected a teacher or got into a fight — he gave you two choices. He could spank you with the paddle or suspend you. I usually took the whupping. Nothing Mr. Kramer could hand out matched what my mother might do.

I was given no option on the day my mom was called in to deal with me. I was in a violent fight. When the teachers tried to break it up, I kept pushing them away and going back after the kid.

I'd crossed the line, Mr. Kramer said. Suspension was the only solution. I knew my mom would have to come get me. I knew what was coming.

My mom was getting ready for work when she received the call. Angry that she was going to be late after dealing with me, she didn't bother getting dressed. It was in between classes, so the hallways were filled with kids when my mom, in her pajamas and carrying a belt, burst through the principal's office door. I was so scared that I didn't even consider how my friends reacted when they saw her.

Mr. Kramer scurried from the room too; he didn't want to witness my mom's fury. It was the worst whupping I ever took. It didn't end in the office either.

Her hands continued to smack me as she yelled at me in the car. Back home, she got in a few more good licks before she went to work.

Did I learn my lesson and stop fighting? Nope. I was spanked so often and by so many people and for things big and small that it meant nothing to me. It was not a deterrence — it was just temporary pain.

Fighting seemed impossible to avoid. I have never sold or done drugs. I have never stolen anything. And although I have never been a bully, I do have one weakness: I hate bullies. As a kid, I hated being bullied, and I hated watching other kids get bullied.

I was 10 years old the first time I was in a physical confrontation. I had an artistic friend who loved to write and draw. He always carried a notebook that he would doodle a drawing or scribble a story in whenever he felt inspired. He was also poor — that notebook was the only one his family could afford. I walked into my classroom at Spadey Elementary one day and saw three kids picking on my friend. They'd stolen his notebook, and, as he demanded it back, they ripped pages and mocked him.

He tried to stand up for himself but was outnumbered.

I had to help.

"Leave him alone," I said.

"It's none of your business," one of the bullies said and ripped another page from the notebook.

"It *is* my business," I screamed. "You wouldn't

like it if someone did something like that to you. What if that was your stuff?"

They kept picking on my friend.

I had no idea if I could fight. I'd never received any formal training — no one in the ghetto had. When the time came, you just knew that you had two options: win the fight or lose the fight.

I didn't sucker punch the bullies — not my style. I walked straight up to one of them, got in his face, and told him to give my friend his notebook or get his butt kicked. He laughed, so I decked him.

He went down. A second bully came after me and didn't do any better. My friend took on the third guy, but then a fourth guy jumped in. Once the first two bullies got up, we were outnumbered and lost the fight.

I wasn't terribly hurt — a few scrapes, some soreness, but no broken bones or deep gashes.

The six of us were sent to the principal's office to be paddled and sentenced to detention. I tried to argue that I was only defending my friend, but Mr. Kramer would have none of that. Fighting was never an option, he said.

When I wasn't defending someone else from bullying, I was being bullied.

Today, people know not to mess with me. No one in their right mind picks a fight with a six-foot-six, 270-pound, muscular man. But back then, as a lanky kid in bad clothes and thick glasses, I was a prime target.

I was cool with neighborhood kids making fun of me. That's just what we did. We all made fun of each other and knew it was nothing personal. We had a relationship. I knew they were just goofing on me and that they respected me, had my back, and would defend me against anyone from outside our circle.

It was different when I was verbally attacked by a random kid at school. Even if the jokes were the same as those from my neighborhood friends, the words were meant to cut me down in public. When that happened, rather than shoot back with insults or walk away, I ended it with violence.

I'd get into pushing matches with kids two to three times a month. At least once every two months, it would escalate, especially if someone dared lay a hand on me. Could I have handled some of the situations peacefully? Sure. But I had no one on in my life to teach me how.

Still, at a school and in a city like mine, sometimes punching the bully in the mouth was the only way to stop him. We had one middle school student who thought he was King Kong. He was my height and had already filled out. He'd walk the hallways and pick on kids as though no repercussions would ever come his way.

I had never had any problems with him, and we rarely talked. Then one day, for no reason and with no warning, he snatched my backpack from my shoulders and emptied the contents on the floor. He then threw the calculator my mom had just bought me, and it smashed into pieces. I knew there was no way she could afford a second. I was mad.

I was lanky, but I was strong. (I've always been strong.) My anger with King Kong then gave me Superman strength.

I knew King Kong wanted to smash me next. So before he could take the first shot, I grabbed him and slung him into a locker. He folded up, and I was on top of him until the teachers broke it up.

Everyone oohing and aahing in that hallway knew I had won that fight. There was no doubt. But the single punch he landed broke one of the arms of my glasses. When I got home, my mom told me we couldn't afford a new pair, and she refused to ask her social worker for help. "You wanna fight and break your glasses, that's on you," she said. "You make those glasses work."

I taped the arm back on, but that made me a bigger target. My glasses were always a source of anxiety for me — I knew I looked goofy. After they broke, I was on edge.

Every so often, I'd try not wearing them, but my mom would punish me if she caught me going to school blind or if she found out I took my glasses off in class. Education trumped whatever kids said about me.

Perhaps to hide my insecurities, I became a class clown. "Get them to laugh at my jokes and not at my looks," I thought. I wasn't the type of class clown who would bring brief moments of levity to the day. I was that obnoxious class clown who, as Charlie Murphy would say, was a habitual line stepper.

I disrupted class with inappropriate jokes, flicked staples, and was a general nuisance. I'd purposely get to class late, push open the door with all my might, and let out a loud burp.

During lunch, I was the kid who started food fights. Teachers would yell at me, and I'd return fire. I had no respect for authority. I stopped trying in school. "Cool kids don't want to be smart," I thought. The bullying had broken me.

I hate bullying. My kids know they should never, ever bully someone. When I mentor kids — especially those from underserved communities — I focus on teaching them to have respect for others.

I am proud to speak at schools and at anti-bullying rallies throughout the country and world through WWE's Be a STAR (Show Tolerance and Respect) campaign. WWE hosts anti-bullying rallies at which we talk about the importance of learning respect, teach lessons about not being a bystander to bullying, and explain the different types of bullying: physical, emotional, verbal, and, new to this generation and the number one type, cyber. We teach them about how to combat it and be a part of the change that eradicates bullying in schools.

Back then, we were told bullying was part of childhood. Suck it up. Fight back. Stand up for yourself. We did that externally. Internally, we were hurting.

Not one time did an adult sit me down and ask why I was lashing out. Would I have immediately said it was because I was being bullied? Probably not. But if they spoke to me with kindness instead of raising their voice to scold me, I would have learned to trust them and eventually opened up to them. I felt like my bullies and the adults in my life were on the same tag team — and their sole mission was to tear me down.

I would hear things like, "With this type of behavior, you're going to end up in jail," or "If you can't control your anger, somebody's going to kill you," or "If you don't focus on academics, you're going to end up selling drugs on the streets." They never said anything positive to me. Their words reinforced my belief that I was a nothing, just some lower-class kid stuck in a bad situation in a life that would only get worse.

Some adults, such as my mom, threatened me with jail and death because they hoped to scare me straight. Others believed that's what would come of me. When verbal whuppings pile up, it is too difficult for a kid to separate the well-intentioned from the bad-intentioned.

Looking back, much of my anger could have been calmed had someone from the outside stepped in earlier to help. I felt second class. We were on the bottom rung of society, in my opinion. That weighs on someone, whether they are a kid or an adult.

My sons, T.J. and Titus, know I love them because I constantly remind them that I do and often tell them that I'm proud of them. I hug them a lot. They know that if I am not working, whatever it is I am doing, I want them with me. Spending time with them is not a fatherhood chore; it's my pleasure and my honor.

When they misbehave, we talk about it. The fact that they know I am disappointed in them is punishment enough. I try not to yell, though I do have my moments. But even when I do, I don't scream, "You're bad!" Instead, I explain why what they did was wrong, and I ask them why they did what they did. Work through the problems — don't shout through the problems. If you are rearing your kids the right way, and they know you love them, there is no need to spank or scream incessantly. The same goes for teachers, coaches, and other types of mentors. The most successful are not those who yell. Rather, they're the ones who show they're more than just authority figures — they take that extra time to relate and show their vulnerabilities, and they never abandon hope.

The moment an adult stops telling a kid to behave better is when they've given up and moved on.

Through the kindness of strangers, though, I did experience moments of feeling like a "normal" kid. They were, unfortunately, short-lived. Still, they were nice.

The only movie I ever saw as a kid living in South Florida was *E.T. the Extra-Terrestrial*. Someone who worked with social services decided to take me and four other kids to the theater and pay for the entire bill. He bought us each our own bag of popcorn, soda, and candy. That was the first time I ever tried Twizzlers — I got hooked. From then on, I bought Twizzlers whenever I had enough change scrounged together. I ate them so much, I can't stomach that candy today. But unlike egg noodles, Twizzlers remind me of good times.

The same goes for Boston baked beans. The first time I tried those was when I was eight years old. It was also the first time I celebrated Halloween. Not only was my neighborhood too rough for trick-or-treating, but this was also during the time when psychos were putting razor blades in apples or poisoning the candy that they were handing out, so my local Boys and Girls Club began hosting indoor trick-or-treating for the surrounding neighborhoods. They'd dress each room in the facility like a different haunted house, give all the kids candy, and serve us dinner: hotdogs and Boston baked beans.

One year, I dressed as a ghost because it was all we could afford. I looked like something out of a *Peanuts* cartoon. That continued to be my costume for the first three years at the Boys Club. I later outgrew wearing costumes, so I went without one. But they still served me those baked beans I loved.

There was also that one Christmas that was almost disastrous for my family. I was 12, and money was so tight, there wasn't going to be a single present under the tree. Ms. Wilfork heard, and she brought me to one of those functions where they give Christmas presents to the less fortunate. A nice woman handed me a remote-controlled car. All these years later, I still remember her words, "I got this just for you because I wanted you to have a nice gift." It was the only present I received that year.

Did that woman specifically buy that remote-controlled car for me? Doubtful. If I had made a Christmas list that year, would a remote-controlled car have been on it? Nope. But her kind words struck a chord with me, and that car remains the best present I ever received as a kid. Whenever I think about it, I think about how special I felt in that moment.

I kept that gift until my junior year of college. The only reason I don't have it today is because my room-mate came home drunk one night and wrecked both my fish tank and that toy. I didn't care about the fish tank, but we fought over that car.

That feeling that someone was thinking about me as an individual and not a faceless poor kid was priceless. Some kids experience that feeling 365 days a year. All kids should, regardless of social class.

Today, I strive to give everyone that feeling.

In 2015, I was in San Diego for a WWE event. I'd just finished eating dinner with some friends when a homeless couple asked for a few dollars to buy a sandwich. I told them I'd do one better. I offered to buy them a sit-down meal at the same restaurant I'd just left.

We walked back to the restaurant, and I told the manager I wanted to buy dinner for the couple. The manager stared at us so uncomfortably that the homeless gentleman got the idea and suggested they take their food to go instead.

"No," I said, "you can eat here like everyone else, and they will treat you with the same dignity they provided to me." I left the manager with more than enough money for their meal, plus a good tip. All I asked was that no alcohol was served to them. The manager agreed.

Fifteen minutes later, something told me to check on them. I found the couple waiting around the corner. They said that after I left, the manager told them to order and then come back later for it in to-go boxes.

I was hot. I went back and demanded to know why the couple was not eating in the restaurant. The manager said they told him they preferred to take the food to go. That was the opposite of what the couple had told me, but I had no proof he was lying. "If that's true," I said, "it's probably because you made them feel uncomfortable." My friends pulled me outside before I made a scene.

Outside, the restaurant's assistant manager chased me down. He apologized and said what I tried to do was admirable.

That meant nothing to me. I asked him if he was

a man of faith and if he believed in God. He said yes. I told him that I expect his faith to be activated the next time he sees unjust behavior. Make sure all people are treated with the love of God, I said, and not as though they are a plague. He agreed.

I made sure the couple received their to-go food and then returned to my hotel.

I stewed in anger all night. I planned on going back to the restaurant, taking a selfie, and blasting them on social media. But when I called my pastor for advice, he told me to do what God would want me to do.

I did exactly that.

The next day, I walked the streets of downtown San Diego for 15 minutes, asking the homeless if they were hungry and, if so, if they wanted a free meal. In all, I gathered 30 homeless people and went back to that same restaurant. The assistant manager met me at the door and set tables for everyone. Watching them eat was fulfilling. Initially, they felt awkward being at that restaurant, being served and eating food that they had long been told was too rich for their taste buds. They didn't feel like they belonged. But by the end of the meal, their insecurities had melted away and they acted no differently than you or I would.

A few years later, in 2018, I led the fundraising effort that raised money to take 3,800 less fortunate Tampa Bay–area kids to see *Black Panther*. I did so for two reasons. One was because I wanted them to see Black men and women portrayed in a positive way — as superheroes — in a movie.

The other reason was because I knew that without someone giving them that opportunity to see that movie at a theater, they would never get to go. I wanted them to have the full experience rather than watch a bootleg copy at home. There were many kids who attended the screenings who told me that it was their first time ever stepping foot inside a movie theater, much like when I went to watch *E.T.*

Buying someone an eight-dollar meal is a great gesture. But buying someone a dining experience or taking them to the movies is even better. It's not so much about the food or the movie, but rather it's about reminding someone that they are not an outcast and, just like everyone else, they're worthy of nice things.

I don't expect you to spend $1,000 to feed 30 homeless people or reach out to non-profits and philanthropists in your area to pay for thousands of kids to see a movie. But if you know a less fortunate child, taking him or her out to dinner or to the movies or a ballgame or an arcade, or to a beach or park that is nicer than the ones they usually go to, could do wonders for their self-esteem. Show them that living in a lower-class neighborhood does not make them lower-class people. Provide them with an opportunity to see life outside of their normal circumstances.

You can even make a difference without spending a penny.

There are many people in this world who want to do something good for children in need, but they think finances, or the lack thereof, hinder them in how much impact they can have on a child's life.

I have come to learn that sometimes the biggest impacts and most impressionable moments are those that require zero finances and instead are provided with genuine love and concern. We often forget that the actions in our lives that we take for granted — a smile, a pat on the back, a question of concern, a listening ear — can mean the world to someone else.

All those things and more can not only help change a person's perspective on life but also empower them.

CHAPTER 3

For the economically disadvantaged children of East Tampa and Ybor City, the Academy Prep Center of Tampa middle school is a haven. Many of the students at the school have one parent, come from households where the next meal is uncertain, and live in neighborhoods where crime flourishes and is always tempting them.

Through need-based scholarships and tremendous donor support, kids attend 11 hours a day, six days a week, 11 months a year. It is more than just a school. It is an extended family meant to keep the kids off the streets and on a path to success. Teachers and administrators seek to show them that there is a different path than the dark one they were exposed to early in life. It provides them with counseling and social services when needed. Post-graduation, the school continues to provide former students the support they need to get into and then graduate from college.

I got involved as an occasional public speaker at Academy Prep when I was playing arena football for the Tampa Bay Storm. When they started a class called Focus on Success, they asked me to be a regular part of it, and I've remained so ever since — 14 years and counting as of the publication of this book. Focus on Success is an eight-week course for the school's seventh graders. It emphasizes envisioning their destination and empowering their beliefs rather than limiting their dreams. A lot of what we do is meant to unbrainwash the kids' false acceptance that the world into which they were born is the only world they deserve.

I let them know that I am proof of that truth.

One exercise we do is have the children close their eyes and visualize that they have everything in life that they could ever want. We tell them to really stretch their imagination because nothing is out of bounds. Their world is a giant box, we tell them, and they can fill that box with presents for themselves, whether those gifts be physical belongings, a certain career, a large family of their own, or anything else.

Once they hit the apex, we have them visualize themselves in a small room with no doors or windows. We describe the room so they feel isolated and alone. Is that their reality? Do they feel claustrophobic?

Then we ask them to expand the walls. We add a window and then another and another. We build a door. We let in fresh air. We have them look out the window and visualize their happy place, whether that is a scenic countryside, exotic island, thriving city, or somewhere else. Finally, we tell them to step out into that world and enjoy its splendors. The point of the exercise is to prove that despite their present circumstances, their future limitations are only in their minds.

The semester culminates with a "Creating Destiny" celebration, a class reunion held 15 years in the future. Each student must come dressed as their future self — as a doctor, lawyer, engineer, or whatever it may be that they envision.

By then, we hope they have shed any preconceived notions they have about themselves, that they can embody their future selves and understand that there is a world beyond their neighborhoods and that it is accessible to them.

I had my first glimpse of the world outside South Florida when, during the summer before eighth grade, Ms. Wilfork — with the help of her friend, the sheriff of Palm Beach County — secured me a spot in a Florida Sheriffs Youth Ranches summer camp. Founded in 1957, the Florida Sheriffs Youth Ranches is a law enforcement–run organization that seeks to battle juvenile delinquency. One way in which they do so is through a free Barberville, Florida, Boys Ranch summer camp for less fortunate kids ages 10 to 15.

Today, it is a co-ed camp for 36 girls and 36 boys. But the summer that Ms. Wilfork enrolled me, it was a boys-only camp, and I would be spending 10 days and nine nights with 99 other boys from low-income areas, most of whom were troublemakers.

At that time, I had never left the South Florida area. So I was bouncing off the walls, ready to go, when Ms. Wilfork told me the summer camp offered activities like camping, canoeing, and archery. It was an adventure from the start — my first road trip. A bus that already had a dozen or so boys from the Miami area picked me up at the local Boys Club and we began our three-hour journey north to Barberville in Volusia County, Florida.

From the moment we left South Florida, my jaw hung in awe and my face was pushed against the window. We drove through miles of winding back roads snuggled between ranches, farms, and thick foliage. I saw horses with their heads hanging over wooden fences and cows grazing in fields in the distance. I'd seen such green before, but only on my family's small television. For a boy who grew up in the cliched concrete jungle, such in-person sights were amazing. My excitement turned to a heavy gulp when we arrived at the 200-acre camp.

The summer camp was a series of dirt roads that connected tent areas, an activities field, a lake, and a "chow hall," a giant screened-in pavilion. For lodging, we each shared a tent with three other boys. It tied shut but didn't zip. To protect us from hand-sized mosquitos, we were each given a bug net to drape over our cots.

The tents were pitched on 12-by-14 wooden platforms lifted a few feet off the ground. But I'd seen enough television to know that wasn't enough protection from snakes. I envisioned them easily slithering into my tent and then my bed. I wasn't alone in my fears; those from the city were whispering their apprehension about the sleeping conditions.

The country boys were fine with it — but I was not, nor was I initially fine with the country boys.

We all had preconceived notions about each other that we later learned were unfair.

I had never been around kids from the country, and they had never been around kids from the projects. I wrongly thought that people who spoke with a southern accent were racist. And from the looks on the white kids' faces, they likely thought that any Black kid from the projects was a thug and a gangbanger.

Still, the camp tossed us all together. That was a purpose of the week: to expose us to new things and new people and to teach us that the world is far different than our limited view of it. Each camping area was broken up by age groups and made up of four tents — three to be split among 12 campers and one for three counselors. A fire pit sat in the middle.

While it may have been a camp run by law enforcement and for less fortunate kids straddling the line of crime and civility, there was nothing prison-like about the place. No one was patted down, and there were no fences to keep us in or armed guards to watch over us. The counselors were in their early twenties, college kids looking to spend their summers doing something positive, and the law enforcement who ran the camp dressed in street clothes. Each campsite was assigned two deputies who stayed with us until we tucked ourselves in at night. That initially gave me pause.

Most of the law enforcement figures I'd seen to that point were those making arrests in my neighborhood. At times, I thought they were unfair or too rough with the local drunks and junkies whose only crime was littering the streets with their passed-out bodies. I'd been wrongfully conditioned to oppose all law enforcement.

But any reservations I had with the camp law enforcement deputies or the southern boys were wiped away by the end of the week.

On the first day, after dinner, the 11-year-old kids sat around our campsite's fire as counselors and deputies laid out the ground rules for the week. Number one dealt with how we spoke to others. Negative words were forbidden. That included more than not being allowed to say things like "you suck." For instance, if someone was walking across a beam of wood a few feet in the air and the person was afraid of heights, yelling "Don't look down" was considered negative, even if we meant it positively. Instead, we were to yell things like, "You can do this," or "There's nothing to worry about."

The counselors and deputies promised that they too would follow that rule. They would not yell or scream. If we got out of line, punishment would be work detail, like cleaning the chow hall or the campsites. If we refused, we'd be sent home. No one would huff or puff at us. We were not being held at the camp against our will.

We were then asked to tell our fellow campers about ourselves. I was too shy to share much at first, so I mumbled that I was from a single-parent home. A counselor pressed for more. "Why are you here this week?" he asked. "I get into trouble a lot at school," I replied. "I need to make better decisions."

I became more at ease when Theron, one of the country boys in my group, told a similar story. "We're from different backgrounds, but maybe we're not all that different," I thought. Then other kids detailed home lives that included awful abuse or explained they were shuffled from foster home to foster home. My life may have been far from perfect, I realized, but I was still luckier than some.

The deputies shared next. They told us about their wives and kids, their childhoods and passions. They let us know that law enforcement officers are people, just like us.

We then sang campfire songs and talked freely amongst ourselves.

As the night turned its darkest, I couldn't help but stare at the sky. I'd been inundated with light pollution throughout my entire life. Back home, I had been privy to only a selection of the countless stars that can be seen from Earth. At that camp, where the only light was coming from our campfires and a few flashlights, I could see them all. I remember thinking that it was the same sky I looked at back home, yet it was so different.

I didn't sleep a minute. Wonder and fear at the sounds of the countryside kept me awake all night. I heard the crickets, the frogs, the owls, and, especially frightening, the wild boars in the distance.

The next morning, a bell the size of the Liberty Bell gonged from the chow hall, and we all got out of our tents to begin our week.

Activities were heavy on team building: Two teammates would have to tie a knot, but each could use only one hand. Or two guys would be tied together and run a football ropes course. There was also a climbing wall that could only be conquered by lifting one teammate onto the wall, who then worked with those on the ground to pull the next kid up. That continued until everyone made it over the wall.

Another game was called "fiery peanut butter." We were taken to a rope-swing course that had multiple platforms set up in a circle, with an imaginary pit of fiery peanut butter in between. Each teammate had to swing from one platform to the next but could not move on to the next platform until everyone was together. Like the wall-climbing exercise, we had to help each kid get to the stand and remain on it without falling off, which became increasingly difficult as it grew more and more crowded.

Counselors stopped us mid-activity if a team member spewed negative comments during the exercise. They reminded us to stay positive and provided us with tips on how to do so, and we started over. If we failed at an activity, it was not an option to shrug our shoulders and say we tried but couldn't do it. We would redo the exercise until we succeeded. They wanted to prove to kids from varying backgrounds that we could succeed at anything if we just worked as a team and put our minds to it.

Other activities that were fun for those country boys jostled the city kids like me out of our comfort zones. Until that week, I'd never touched a worm, let alone baited a hook — my grandmother had always taken care of that for me. But counselors handed me a fishing pole, stood me near the water, and gave me two choices — fish on my own or watch the other kids. I stared at the worms wiggling around that basket for a few minutes and then plunged my hand inside. It was gross, but I grabbed one and stuck it on my hook before I could talk myself out of it. Later that day, I caught a catfish. It is the nastiest type of fish you can reel in, and I threw it back rather than cook it as the country boys would have. Still, it was a fish nonetheless, and the first I'd ever caught all on my own.

Kayaking played out in the same manner. I thought they were crazy when they showed me that long watercraft and told me to cram my body into it and paddle down De Leon Springs. "Black kids from the projects don't do that type of thing," I rationalized. But that was the point. They needed me to realize I was not a Black kid from the ghetto. I was a kid with no limitations.

Before the journey began, they told us not to panic no matter what happened. Easier said than done. I had a life vest on, but I freaked out when the kayak flipped over and caught me upside down underwater. I thought I was going to drown. The counselors got to me quickly and rolled the kayak over. When I realized I was safe, I thought, "Alright, alright, I didn't die. I got this." The physical act of kayaking was easy, I realized; it was my fear and self-doubt that had made it difficult. I could do it once my anxiety was gone.

I also learned how to ride a horse and shoot a bow and arrow, and the deputies brought us to a campsite shooting range to teach us how to shoot a .22 rifle.

And the food — oh the food! It was all homemade. I'd never eaten that well for so many days in a row in my life. Breakfasts included scrambled eggs, pancakes, waffles, French toast, orange juice, fruit, bacon, and sausage. Lunch was usually a hardy sandwich with chips. Dinner was the best — roast beef with mashed potatoes and gravy, or chicken and dumplings, freshly prepared right in front of our eyes before it was plopped on our plates. Dessert was served every night — pecan pie, apple pie, and even hot fudge sundaes!

At night, we'd gather around our site's campfire to talk about our days: what we did, how we fared, what we overcame. We were not allowed to focus on the lows — only the highs. At the beginning of the week, a counselor or a deputy would turn the conversation to focus on the positives of the day when someone failed to do so, but by the end of the week, that role had been taken over by the campers. We'd tell a boy who was down on himself why he should be proud. Our attitudes had performed a complete 180-degree transformation from when we had arrived.

The counselors and deputies would also ask us about our favorite sports teams or comic book characters, and when someone from a different background had the same likes or dislikes, it reinforced that we were not all that different.

One night, the entire camp gathered together for skits. Each site teamed with their deputies to perform their show. I cannot recall exactly what we did, but I remember looking at the deputies — whom I did not fully trust earlier in the week — as role models.

The week concluded with a graduation ceremony. It was the only time the deputies were in full uniform. We all gathered at the chow hall, and the deputies drove up in a parade of squad cars, lights and sirens blaring, as we all cheered in excitement.

They handed out an award to each kid for something they'd accomplished during their stay. Unfortunately, I don't remember what my award was, but I'd guess it was something to do with being a camp clown. Of course, I wasn't a perfect angel that week. I was my usual goofy self who cracked jokes, clowned around, and messed with others. But, as promised, no one yelled or demeaned me in any way. No one weaponized my background by proclaiming if I didn't listen, I'd end up in prison or dead. They instead stayed positive and drilled into my head that, if I so chose, I was bound for success.

Their approach worked. If I was being a pest, it never morphed beyond silliness.

And the camp had Black kids, white kids, Latinx kids; kids who'd been abused mentally, physically, sexually, or all three; kids with criminal records of all kinds; kids from single-parent homes, kids with two parents, and kids who had bounced from foster home to foster home. Yet, there was no violence. We all got along.

I learned the value of teamwork and team building. If I could go to a new place and meet strangers from different backgrounds yet find a way to make things work, I wondered why I couldn't do that all the time. I realized that not all people were out to get me and that there are other kids out there who were just like me. I even realized that there were some people who were worse off than I was. I wasn't alone.

And I realized there was an entire world out there beyond what I'd known prior to camp. When you come from a certain situation and never have a moment to escape it, you believe that is what your entire world will always be like — you think that your small bubble will remain your globe. The whole experience gave me a different perspective. For those 10 days, I felt like I was worth something.

Today, I take that belief with me all throughout the world, and especially to my special place, Academy Prep.

One of the exercises we do during the Focus on Success class is called "twinning." I play one twin, and another adult pretends to be the other. We tell the kids that we were raised by a father who was so abusive and such an alcoholic that we were sent to the foster system that bounced us from home to home. One of us goes down the wrong road, turns to crime, and ends up incarcerated. The other one goes to college, earns a degree, has a family, and starts his own successful business.

We then let the kids ask us questions about our lives, so that they can figure out why we turned out so differently.

At first, the kids typically want to know things like if the good brother ever tried to help the bad brother and when the last time we talked was. At some point, a kid will ask us, point-blank, "Why do you each feel like you turned out the way you did?" We always reply in unison, "With a dad like I had, I didn't have any other choice."

One twin uses his upbringing as an excuse for failure. The other sees it as motivation to succeed.

CHAPTER 4

April 17, 2018. King Abdullah International Stadium, Jeddah, Saudi Arabia.

It is the *Greatest Royal Rumble* — a 50-man over-the-top rope battle royal in front of 60,000 screaming fans. This is the type of event entertainers dream about. I am pumped.

I'm entrant 39. My music hits. It's Titus Worldwide Time. I sprint from the backstage area into the arena and down the aisle. My plan is to slide into the ring at full speed, start kicking some butt, get a pop from the crowd, and make a lasting impression.

But as I get a few feet from the ring, it happens. I hit a wet spot on the ground, and instead of sliding into the ring, I slip and slide under it.

There was a pop alright, but it was laughter from the crowd.

As I lay in the darkness, my first reaction was to make sure I was not hurt. (I was fine.) Then it hit me — I had just made one of the most epic blunders in the history of WWE and had done so in front of the tens of thousands of fans inside the arena and the millions watching around the world.

I got up, entered the ring as though nothing happened, and did my job.

A few minutes later, Braun Strowman eliminated me. Once backstage, as expected, those in the locker room clowned me for my trip and fall. But it didn't end there.

Footage of my slip went viral. Dubbed the "Titus World Slide," it was shared all over social media with comedic background music. It became a meme. ESPN showed it on *SportsCenter* so many times that it made the 2018 NOT Top 10 Plays of the Year list, finishing at a strong number six.

The next night on *Monday Night Raw*, WWE's flagship program televised weekly on the USA Network, WWE and I decided to make it part of my storyline. I wore a "Titus World Slide" shirt and pretended the trip was on purpose. I was again stricken by clumsiness later that night.

I don't take myself too seriously. You play a superhero on TV, but in real life you are still just human, and humans make mistakes. You need to laugh at your mistakes rather than harp on them. If you get up with confidence, no one else will harp on it either.

I did not get down on myself about the fall. Why should I have? I wasn't injured, and there have been other people who have slipped on even bigger stages, and they turned out just fine.

While I will be a part of WWE blooper packages for decades to come, the most memorable moment from that night, which included other Superstars, such as John Cena, Rey Mysterio, Randy Orton, Triple H, and Undertaker, is the Titus World Slide . . . I basically stole the show.

No matter what your profession or passion is, you have to remember to focus on what you need to do next to succeed rather than dwelling on failures of your past. Those who have been truly successful in life — whether as an athlete, businessman, lawyer, politician, scientist, entertainer, or whatever else — reached that pinnacle only after they had been knocked down hundreds of times.

Look at Tom Brady. Everyone considers him to be either the greatest or one of the greatest quarterbacks to ever play professional football. He wasn't taken until the sixth round of the NFL draft — the 199th pick overall — and played behind a great quarterback, Drew Bledsoe, whom most pundits believed he would never start over. He could have sulked and had a woe is me attitude. Instead, he focused on what he needed to do to make himself a better player and, when Bledsoe went down, he was prepared. By the way — Brady was number *seven* on ESPN's 2018 NOT Top 10 list for looking uncoordinated as a wide receiver on a trick play. It goes to show that at any point, even a G.O.A.T. can become the goat.

Then there's the most famous protagonist of this kind of story: Michael Jordan. He was cut from his high school basketball team, but rather than giving up, he used that memory as fuel to improve.

Everybody falls at some point — sometimes literally. It's just a matter of how you get back up. You'll succeed more times than not if you get up with confidence and soldier on. Of course, maybe I was able to bounce back from the Titus World Slide so quickly because I had experience in athletic failure.

Let's rewind three decades. I'm 10 years old and playing nose guard for my peewee football team. It was third down, late in the fourth quarter, and the opposing team was driving down the field. The quarterback tossed the ball to the running back, who headed for the open field. I raced after him, desperate to keep him from reaching that first-down marker. He tried to shake me. Instead, he fell face first into the ground with me on top of him. My teammates celebrated like we'd just won the Super Bowl.

It was the highlight of my athletic career up to that point. It was also my only accomplishment.

Here is the rest of the story about that tackle. It was week six. We were blowing the other team out. That was the first time I'd gotten into a game that season. I didn't so much make a tackle as the running back tripped and fell over, and I jumped on top of him. My teammates were not celebrating in earnest. They were more so overdoing it in jest for the benchwarmer they mockingly called "Eyes," for the thick glasses I wore.

I went with it. As they whooped it up, so did I, jumping up and down like I'd made the game-winning tackle during a crucial moment.

I got into the game again the next week. Again, it was late in the fourth quarter, and we were winning in a blowout. I made another tackle — a real one that time — and the team cheered again. The play-offs started the following week, and I didn't leave the sidelines again that season.

There was nothing about me that season that would have led people to believe that one day I'd become an All-American high school football player who'd later start for the University of Florida and then become a WWE Superstar. Still, joining that peewee team was a turning point in my life.

In the projects, where no one has the money to go anywhere or do anything extravagant, you make do with what you have. To have fun, all we needed was a football so we could play throw 'em up, blow 'em up.

We played on the concrete but hit each other like we were on mattresses. Skin tore from our arms and legs. Heads slammed against the pavement. When the ball was accidentally thrown into a tree and bounced from branch to branch, we pretended that we wanted to catch it, but, really, we were each praying it would fall into someone else's arms because we knew that whoever got it, got it.

My mom's boyfriend and my brothers' father, Clifford, knew how much I loved football, and shortly before he left us, he suggested I sign up to play for the Delray Rocks peewee team. It was the only positive thing Clifford ever did for me. Playing for the Delray Rocks was a big deal. They put power-houses on the field.

Those teams were a great sense of pride for a community of minorities who had very little. The Rocks were something everyone rallied behind.

Dads didn't coach the teams. We were not led by a bunch of dudes who wished they'd played bigtime football and were living vicariously through the kids. Coaches had legitimate knowledge of the game and ran practices like drill sergeants. And they were not one-and-done coaches. The same adults — a mix of community leaders like teachers, law enforcement, and preachers — were involved with the Delray Rocks for years and years.

When big games rolled around, hundreds of people sat in the bleachers and surrounded the field.

My mother worked concessions during games to offset some of the league costs. My mom's social worker Barbara Wilfork's family took me to the field if my mom had to work late.

You may have heard of Mrs. Wilfork's son: Vince Wilfork, the retired nose guard who won two Super Bowls for the New England Patriots.

I'm five years older than he is, so we were not on the same team, but all the squads practiced at the same sports complex in Delray Beach. Vince and I remain friends to this day. We're not super close, but he's always a phone call away, and I remain forever in debt to his mother for all she did for my mom and my family. She'd come by my house a lot — sometimes to check on my mom, sometimes to make sure we had enough food, sometimes to ask how I was doing in school and if I was staying out of trouble. Her personality was rich and very motherly. She was a stern woman, and when I screwed up, she matter-of-factly told me so.

Her husband, David, a maintenance worker for the Palm Beach County recreation department, was a little more standoffish. He was more of the "I'm here if you need me — if not, then cool" type of guy rather than a "I'm here to be your mentor" type of guy. I respected the hell out of that man just because he was an active father to both his sons. He was everything I envisioned a father should be. When he spoke, I listened.

Because I was so big for my age, I did not play on a team with my friends. I had to play on a squad made up of kids who were two and three years older than I was. They'd already grown into their bodies, whereas I was still searching for my balance. Plus, at that age, two to three years is like decades in terms of mental maturity. Making the team was one thing. I realized early on that getting playing time was going to be an entirely separate battle.

That was a tough pill to swallow.

Practices were grueling. We ran hard. We hit hard. We did it all in the Florida heat.

I love football now and loved it then. I love being in an atmosphere where you're getting your ass handed to you and you must use every ounce of strength in your body to kick someone's ass back. I think everyone in the hood is wired that way. When you have to fight for everything you get, you grow up harder than those who have life handed to them.

Still, I was a little kid that first season. It wasn't always easy making it through those practices knowing there was little chance I'd play a snap in a game. I'd goof off or not practice as hard as I could. I had the attitude that it didn't really matter what I did since I wouldn't be part of that week's game anyway. Then one night, as Mr. Wilfork was driving Vince and me home from our practices, he laid into his son for clowning around.

"Look, we are paying a lot of money for you to

be out there," he said, "the least you can do is show up. And if you don't show up, I'm gonna show you out." Not working your hardest is a disservice to those who support you, he told Vince.

That sunk in for me. A neighborhood dad gave me cleats. My mom, who served food all day, was then doing it again during games. The Wilforks were driving me to practices. A lot of people were making sacrifices so that I could be on the Delray Rocks. Even if I never played one snap, I needed to play hard and focus out of respect for them.

I've since given the same lecture to too many kids to count. I've told my sons that their coaches should never come to me after practice and say, "Your son did not practice hard," or "Your son was late to practice," or "Your son has stopped giving his best effort." I can deal with anything else. If a coach says a kid is not that great of an athlete but he works his ass off, that's fine. But if a coach says the reverse, "That kid is a great athlete, but he's lazy," then that is a recipe for failure.

You don't have to have an athletic bone in your body to play sports, I remind kids. When you try your best, neither you nor anyone else can be disappointed. The reason why I'm in the position I am in today is not because I am the most talented or the best. It's because my work ethic can never be questioned.

When raising, teaching, or mentoring kids, applaud work ethic just as much as you do talent.

Praise character more than you praise statistics. Preach teamwork over superstardom.

Our coaches for the Delray Rocks had that attitude. They didn't place winning before grooming boys into men. How we acted off the field was more important to them than how we performed on the field.

The head coach was Matthew "Bump" Mitchell, a Delray legend whose story has been well chronicled. He earned his nickname as an undersized high school quarterback. The only thing his center could see when he looked back to hike the ball was the top of Coach Mitchell's head, which looked like a bump. After high school, he worked as a janitor for the Palm Beach County School Board while moonlighting as an auxiliary police officer in Delray. He later earned a full-time position on the force, was eventually promoted to sergeant, and preached at Christ Missionary Baptist Church.

As an officer, Coach Bump had a reputation for having a soft spot for juvenile delinquents. Instead of arresting a kid, he was known to take the child to his office for a lecture. He'd seek to mentor the child rather than have him face a judge, and if you played for his team, off-field indiscretions were further punished on the field. On some occasions, he'd penalize the team for one player's behavior. After a grueling practice, we'd be kept late to run even more conditioning drills as he reminded everyone that it was the team's duty to keep each player in line.

When report cards came out, players with bad grades had to lay on their backs in the cockroach position for nearly the entire practice. After practice, they got their licks — one swipe for every bad grade. Coach Bump always found the biggest switch he could. Still, while he never spared the rod, he didn't yell. He lectured in a stern voice, but he never screamed or demeaned us. He reminded us that we all had potential, and failing to live up to it was a sin.

Coach Bump's demeanor was like Tony Dungy's, the former NFL coach who was famous for keeping a level head. His assistant coach, Coach Stephens, was like Nick Saban, the current Head Coach of the Alabama Crimson Tide, who is famous for the opposite reason. That man would yell, hoot, holler, and get hot. He had no problem dressing you down.

Realizing this, my mom would go to him when I became too disrespectful at home.

Not only would Coach Stephens punish me with further conditioning drills, he'd give me an earful the entire practice. If I was run over during a play, he'd yell, so the whole team could hear, "Keep talking to your mama like that and that's gonna keep happening!" If I jumped offside, he'd scream, "You got no discipline at home and you got no discipline on the field!"

But he didn't just dress us down and then let us leave practice. He always made sure to build us back up first. He understood we needed tough love, but that we also needed to know we were loved.

If I made a great play later in practice, he'd tell me in a fatherly voice, "We know you can do more of that. You just have to apply yourself and be consistent. That's why you're here, and that's why you made the team. Everybody can contribute." If I didn't make a play worthy of a compliment, he'd still let me know that he was proud of me for working hard.

Coach Stephens also had a bad stutter that he never let hold him back. Instead, he'd use it as a teaching tool. Despite his speech impediment, he was a confident public speaker and communicator. When he'd see that I was down after teammates mockingly called me "Eyes," he'd purposely stutter a bit more and tell me, "It doesn't matter what you look like or how you talk. All that matters is the man you are." I respected the hell out of Coach Stephens.

The coaches didn't play favorites either. If a star player got into trouble before a big game, they'd get benched. And if we lost that game, the coaches would let us know that it was because that star had let the team down.

Coach Bump and Coach Stephens were aware of the types of kids they were grooming. Most of us came from tough situations. The coaches wanted to make sure that our success on the football field was not the last success we had in life. They drilled into our heads that it was not about having one good practice or one good report card; it was about consistency. They wanted to instill a good work ethic and valuable habits into every player on the team. And, luckily for me, they refused to give up on any player, no matter what.

While the Boys Ranch camp had a positive impact on me in the short term, it had a negative impact on me in the long term. I had experienced a taste of another life that I figured I'd never touch again. I was hungrier than ever for that life. That hunger turned to frustration.

Throughout the eighth grade, I clashed horribly with my teacher, Ms. Butler, who was always yelling at me. Truth be told, she had every right to be hard on me. I was a jerk.

I brought my greatest hits to her class. I'd stand outside her door as the rest of the class filed into her room. Moments after the bell rang for class to start, I'd barge in — purposely late — and let out a loud burp. Once in my seat in the back of the room, I'd interrupt class with inappropriate jokes, tap my fingers on other kids' desks just to get under their skin, and find other creative ways to act generally disruptive.

I'd play pencil break with my friends. That's a two-person game in which one player holds horizontally between both hands a pencil that the opponent attempts to break with the flick of another pencil. The players alternate turns, and the first one to break the opponent's pencil wins. It was a fun game. But it was not appropriate to play during class.

Was I the only misbehaved kid in that class? No. But of all those kids, I was doing the worst academically. So while Ms. Butler was willing to give the other misbehaved kids some slack, I was on a short leash.

At the time, I didn't understand why she was treating me the way she did. In my mind, I was a victim. Not only did I think Ms. Butler yelled at me too much, I felt like she was trying to embarrass me by calling me out in front of the class. She would often ask me questions she knew would stump me. Sometimes she'd ask me to solve a problem on the blackboard in front of everyone. Today, I realize she was trying to get through to me. She hoped that I would try to best her by studying.

But I was too defiant. Instead of conforming, I'd lash out more. It became a control issue for me. She wanted to prove it was her class; I wanted to prove it was my class. "I may not run it," I thought, "but I sure as hell will dictate when she can teach."

Now, it's easy to say that maybe she should have tried to find another way to reach me besides yelling at me and embarrassing me. But looking back on it, who's to say that she knew any other way. She just saw a kid with potential whom she thought she could help, and that was how she'd always gone about reaching such kids. I don't fault her for trying to make a difference. I just wasn't in a place where I could accept it.

As the school year went on, the tension between us grew, until it came to a head during the final week before winter break. We were taking a test that I didn't feel like doing, so I christmas-treed the answers, meaning I just filled in random bubbles, and put my head down for a nap.

Knowing it was impossible for even a stellar student — let alone a lackadaisical one like me — to finish the test so quickly, Ms. Butler dug her nails into my wrist and began shaking me awake.

To this day, I have no idea why I reacted the way I did. I jerked my head up, grabbed a soft-covered book that sat on my desk, and flung it toward Ms. Butler. It didn't slam into her, but it grazed her shoulder. That was enough. Except for a few whispers of "Why would he do that?" the class was silent. No one oohed or aahed — my fellow students were in total shock. I knew I had screwed up.

Ms. Butler was not normally intimidating. She was slender and had blond hair with a hint of gray. But in that moment, she resembled the Wicked Witch of the West. Doing everything she could to contain her rage, Ms. Butler clenched her jaw and demanded, "Get. Out. Now. Go. To. The. Office."

To make sure I went, she had one of the do-gooder students walk me to the principal.

Normally, I needed a chaperone because I wouldn't go to the office immediately without one. I'd walk the hallways and screw around a bit to prove I was my own boss. But there was no need to have anyone shadow me on that day. I'd messed up bad enough. I wasn't going to compound it.

At the time, my principal was Ms. Payne, a five-foot-two dark-skinned woman with curly hair who did not mess around. She let students know what was on her mind, explained how they disappointed her, and then came down with a harsh yet fair sentence. I knew that I faced possible expulsion. What I did not expect was the extent to which Ms. Payne lost her temper. She didn't normally yell, but on that day, she blew her top.

"What were you thinking?" she demanded.

I tried to say it was an accident, but with my history as a troublemaker and a violent student, she did not believe me for one second.

"I can't have this," she said. "You need to go home. Your school year might be over."

She called my mom, but she was getting ready for work and refused to come. Just days earlier, my mother had lectured me that she was on the verge of losing her job because of how many times she had been late to work or had to leave mid-shift to come deal with me at school. Earnestly afraid that she'd be fired, she called Coach Bump.

Ms. Payne didn't tell me who was coming to pick me up, but as I waited, she repeatedly said, "You're probably going to jail for this." I don't know if she said this to scare me because she knew Coach Bump, who was in law enforcement, was coming or if she truly believed that.

I was shocked when Coach Bump walked in. Without addressing why he was there, he matter-of-factly told me to stand up to be cuffed. "You're going down to the jailhouse with me," he said.

I cried. I had spent the past few years creating the persona of a tough guy who didn't care about anything other than goofing around, but that facade melted away and gave way to who I really was — a kid. I was not a thug, a criminal, or a bad kid. I was just a regular kid — a very scared regular kid.

I bowed my head in shame as he marched me through the hallways past my peers. For years, teachers and other adults told me I'd end up in jail. There I was, proving them right.

Coach Bump remained silent for the first few minutes of our drive. Then, without taking his eyes off the road, he said in his firm tone, "Is this the life you want? Because if it is, this is where you'll end up."

"No, sir," I said, my usual too cool attitude long gone.

"Well, then why would you think it was OK to do what you did?" he asked.

I said nothing.

"You do not belong in jail," he said. "But if you do not change your ways, you will end up there. Or worse, you could end up dead. I don't want that for you."

At the station, he uncuffed me and escorted me into a holding cell. He made it clear I was not under arrest, but he reminded me, "This is where you are at risk of ending up again and again," and left me there alone for hours.

When Coach Bump informed me that I'd still be going to practice that night, I knew my punishment would continue . . .

Admittedly, I had mixed feelings when I got to the field. Part of me was ashamed of what I'd done, but part of me also felt cool. Throwing a book at a teacher would up my street cred, I figured. But Coach Bump Quickly verbally beat me into submission in his low-key way, and the team had his back rather than mine. He rounded up the team and explained, "We had a situation today. I had to bring Thaddeus downtown. *I'm* not going to tell you why — *he* is."

After I murmured my story, the team didn't think I was a cool kid who refused to let a teacher tell him what to do. Instead, they were upset at my lack of respect and explained I'd have to earn my way back onto the team. That night, on top of extra conditioning, I also became the team's crash test dummy during tackling drills. It remained that way for weeks.

I had more punishment to come. My mom lectured me during the entire drive home from practice. Once home, she doled out a whupping. None of that phased me. By that time, I was numb to both verbal and physical punishment. I knew I'd screwed up. I was just ready to move on.

I was not expelled, but I was suspended for the final few days of the term. My mother couldn't take time off work to look after me, and she was afraid I'd get into more trouble if I was left home alone, so she arranged for Coach Bump to step in.

Each morning, he'd pick me up at home, cuff me, place me in the back of his police car, drive me to the station, escort me into a holding room, and have me spend the day writing sentences. I filled pages with phrases like, "I will show more self-control," "I will make something of myself," and "I will make better decisions."

Every so often he'd check on me, grab my completed sentences, and rip them to shreds. You read that correctly. He had me write pages of sentences just so he could tear them up.

I wanted to fight him so bad after he did it the first time.

Instead, I dejectedly asked, "What's the point of all this?"

"When you make bad decisions, whatever you do next won't matter to people," he said.

It was hard for me to understand that at that time because I was so upset, but I get it now. If I repeated something enough, even in punishment, I was less likely to repeat that action and more likely to remember the consequences of that action and learn the lesson behind why what I did was wrong.

He also said, "Every time you get into trouble, a police officer has to write, a principal has to write, or teachers have to write about your unnecessary actions. They must write a police report, a referral. They have to follow up with counselors. You're wasting people's time because you don't want to listen, all because you want to be a class clown, all because you want to make people laugh, all because you want to fight. How funny is it now? How tough are you now? You're the one who's doing the paperwork, and somebody is taking your paper and literally ripping it up in front of your face."

During my few days at the station, the only time I left that holding room was for bathroom breaks. The timing was always too perfect to be a coincidence. As I was led to the bathroom, someone — a drunk, a strung-out drug addict, a gang member — would always be getting booked at that same moment.

Seeing that and being cooped in a room by myself like a prisoner hit home for me that I never wanted to go to jail. But did I walk out of that police station on my final day a changed young man who was ready to turn his life around? Was I "scared straight"? Not at all. Still, it impacted me in the same way that every adult who tried to help me impacted me.

For as long as I can remember, I was a disrespectful kid with a violent streak. I was a problem. And all things considered, my life could have turned out very differently. I could have become an addict. I could have sold drugs or lashed out with guns rather than fists. But for some reason, I never for a moment considered embracing those immoral ways.

Why?

Again, I am not a psychologist or a psychiatrist, but from my life experience, this is my opinion: in the nature versus nurture debate, I side with nurture. Luckily for me, I had adults willing to nurture me. They provided me with a good moral compass.

Think back to the twinning exercise. There are a lot of kids across the globe who are in a bad situation, day in and day out. They see their mom being physically abused. They watch their parents in a toxic marriage, cussing each other out. Some think such behavior is OK, and it's normal if they act out in that manner.

Others, however, look at such people and decide that they will be nothing like them, even if they don't realize it. Someone provided them with that moral compass.

Remember, I don't drink enough to get drunk because I don't ever want to be compared to my brothers' father. Because I was bullied, I am the exact opposite of a bully — I defend those who are picked on.

When I walked outside as a kid, I'd see people passed out on corners. I could have just accepted that that was how I'd end up; instead, I told myself I would never end up like that. I would be like Coach Bump, Coach Stephens, or the Wilforks. When I walked into a room, I wanted to be greeted with respect.

Everyone in this world will come to that cross-roads at some point in their life. They will have to decide which twin they will be. Will they be the twin who mimics the deadbeat dad or the twin who wants to be everything his father is not. Kids with good role models will have an easier time choosing the right path.

Everybody falls at some point, it's just a matter of how you get back up. Not only does that refer to how you deal with yourself, it also refers to how you deal with others. If you're drawn toward a kid and you want to become their mentor, you cannot walk away when things get tough.

Our society's greatest heroes are our teachers, coaches, counselors, and anyone who takes the time to groom kids into fine adults at our schools and universities.

I have even higher respect for those who do so at

the Title I schools, which receive supplemental government funds because they have a high percentage of students from low-income households. Those individuals aren't just charged with educating students, they also have to handle all the baggage that comes with working with such kids, and they do it without the necessary funding to properly tackle the task.

I talk to a lot of those teachers, and they admit that there are days when they don't want to go to work. There are days when they feel like they do not have the tools to make a difference for those students. Or, even with the tools, teachers are unsure if some kids can be reached because they are in such a bad place mentally. But those same teachers also tell me that they make it through the tough days by reminding themselves that there is a big difference between what they feel and what they know.

Feelings change constantly. You can have a big blow up with your spouse and go to bed feeling like you hate them. But when you wake up, you remember that you love them.

Title I professionals choose to work with such kids because they know that all kids can be taught and can be reached. Sometimes, trying to reach people and help people can almost feel like you are on a hamster wheel.

When you hit that point, try to take a step back and get another perspective from a person who has experience in dealing with such situations. The reality is that a person in need will have a vastly different point of view. Therefore, perhaps the approach must be vastly different than what you tried. Sometimes the best approach comes from the viewpoint of others who have experience living through the same difficult situation as the person you are trying to reach.

For instance, you might take a child or a person in need out to a nice restaurant to show them a different side of the world. But you may not be aware that that person has no idea how to order from a menu, why the fork, knife, and spoon are placed a certain way, and has no table etiquette of any kind, all because they are a stranger to that situation.

You proceed to try to teach them but have little to zero success. Your frustration rises until you finally give up and just let that person eat how they want to eat and act how they want to act. And then you leave the restaurant and say, "Well I tried, but it didn't work," and then you are discouraged from trying that again with either that person or someone like them.

Rather than being discouraged, though, you should be encouraged by the fact that you provided an opportunity, even if it did not go the way you hoped.

Now, the hard part — expanding from that opportunity, learning from it, and growing from it. Just like you want them to learn and grow, you must learn and grow.

Talk to them before you go to that restaurant again. Ask them if they've ever been out to eat, even if you know the answer. Then you can lessen your expectation regarding what they know and explain what is expected of them. Don't aim for perfection, but improvement.

Also, seek out someone else to join you, perhaps a friend or a co-worker, and explain the first experience to them so that they can help you develop a different approach. If that fellow diner comes from similar circumstances as the person you are trying to teach, even better. Ask them what it was like the first time they ate at a nice restaurant. Were they scared? Were they overwhelmed? Were they aware what the uses of the different spoons and forks were? How did they learn? What was done to help them feel at ease?

Open your mind to those suggestions. Step outside of your thoughts and step into the thoughts of others, including the one you are trying to help.

If you take these steps, while it may not go exactly the way you would like it to go, it will go better than the time before.

This is progress.

This is the approach that many successful teachers, counselors, coaches, and mentors I know take to reach those children and families in need. If they all gave up the first time, when change was not immediate, they would never make progress.

My pastor used to say, "Blessings delayed are not blessings denied." The progress you are trying to make might be delayed, but that doesn't mean you should give up. It means you need to keep trying and keep looking for different ways to accomplish your mission.

I can't repeat this enough — mentoring kids with tough backgrounds can be hard. There are going to be moments when it feels like nothing you say or do is helping them. But remember, when you first connected with that kid, it was because something inspired you, and you knew you could reach him or her. Maybe the kid isn't overtly responding yet, but, trust me, you are benefiting the child.

Adult after adult failed to get me to totally change my ways. Adult after adult fell down while trying. But they never gave up. They kept getting back up. And while early in my life, they may not have been able to get me to completely turn over a new leaf, they provided me with the moral compass that prevented me from taking things too far.

CHAPTER 5

Maybe you've heard the old proverb, "Give a man a fish, and you feed him for a day; teach a man to fish, and you feed him for a lifetime." It's my belief that we should take this saying to heart — and go further.

Teach a poor man to fish, and you give him an occupation that will feed him for a lifetime. He will teach his kids to fish. His kids might start a chartering business that affords them to buy a home and send their kids to college. Some of those kids will grow that chartering business into a major company, others will go off to college and become doctors and lawyers and engineers and astronauts. That once poor family is then well-off and, remembering their humble roots and knowing someone once helped their ancestors, they use their riches to uplift others in their community, which starts that same upward cycle for countless other families.

Giving a man a fish is transactional. Teaching that man to fish is transformational.

In our society, we are dedicated to transactional changes but not dedicated enough to effect transformational change. That's likely because the former is much easier. I love Thanksgiving, and it is wonderful that people give out turkeys every year, as well as presents on Christmas. These are kind and necessary gestures that address short-term needs, but they are transactional. Let's keep doing that, but let's also do more to incite transformational change.

Some families might say, "Great, I will eat today and will have leftovers to last a few more days, but after that I'll be back in the same place I was before Thanksgiving." Don't mistake such reactions as ingratitude. Rather, realize that eating is a necessity for all people, and for those who don't know where their next meal is coming from, it is something they are always thinking about. At the same time, they're just as concerned with how they are going to permanently get out of their hole. The belief that all homeless or poor people are lazy is a false stereotype. They want to get out of that situation, but they need assistance. They need access to services that provide job training, affordable housing, and educational opportunities, which will help them to rebuild their lives. Then, once on stable footing, some will pay it forward by volunteering at those same services.

The summer camp I attended was a transactional gesture that provided me a short-term break from the issues I faced. If you had told childhood me that I could go to that camp every summer, I would have readily said yes, please. Every summer, I would have enjoyed that respite from life in South Florida, and at the end of camp, I'd return to the environment that was the root of my problems. I would have never transformed.

This is why I believe, despite the lessons I learned at the camp, I remained the angry, book-flinging kid. It's why even after I was suspended and was taught those lessons by Coach Bump, I returned to school and fell back into the same patterns — fighting, disrespecting adults, and goofing around in class. Nothing was going to change for me unless I could get a change of scenery. I didn't see any path to success in Boynton Beach, so I accepted failure.

Then, in March 1991, a prospect for change emerged.

I didn't say much to my mom about what I'd experienced at summer camp. But based on the few things I did tell her, she knew I enjoyed it. She passed that sentiment on to Mrs. Wilfork, who sought to replicate my summer camp experience on a full-time basis — at the Florida Sheriffs Boys Ranch in Live Oak, a three-hour drive from Tampa.

Run by the same non-profit that manages the summer camp, the Boys Ranch is a long-term residential program for at-risk youth. It takes kids from both privately placed families and community-based care agencies. The majority of the kids go there because, like me, they are struggling. They have behavior issues, they have family issues, and they have academic issues. It is not a place for kids who are already breaking the law and who have become a danger to society. Rather, it's a place for those kids who are straddling that line but, if given the right guidance, have the potential to become upstanding and contributing citizens. The Boys Ranch teaches work ethic, self-control, respect, and spirituality through love rather than discipline.

It was a Friday when Mrs. Wilfork talked to me about moving to the Boys Ranch. If I was interested, she'd arrange a tour for Monday. She told me it was just like the summer camp, except I'd sleep in an air-conditioned cottage and go to school during the day.

To say I was excited is an understatement.

When we got to the ranch, that excitement turned into intimidation.

The ranch sits on 3,200 acres that straddle the Suwannee River. Only 400 acres are part of the actual ranch; the rest is made up of miles upon miles of thick forest. It's run by law enforcement personnel, but, like the summer camp, there are no bars or armed guards. Yet there is no escaping, either.

"Civilization is a fifteen-minute drive in every direction," ranch administration often said, chuckling as they told tales of kids who had tried to run away, only to return later that day or the next.

It is an actual operational ranch. They had and still have around 50 horses and 300 to 350 head of cattle grazing in the pastures. There are no crops, but they do harvest hay.

The kids work the ranch — collecting hay, helping in the mechanic shop, fixing fences, tending to sick cattle and pregnant cows, whatever needs to be done. Today, the ranch is co-ed. When I was there, it was a space for 100 troubled boys.

It was and is a total culture shock for any kid from the city. I've heard stories about boys who came to the camp having never before seen a cow and some who thought cattle were horses with horns. I wasn't that naive, but it was the first time I'd seen a cow up close or had ever smelled manure first thing in the morning. For a city boy, *that* took some getting used to.

I was a little hesitant after the tour of the ranch. Plus, the reality of the situation had hit me. The ranch was more than 200 miles from home. And, unlike the summer camp, I would not be leaving in 10 days. The ranch keeps kids until they are emotionally steady and their home life is stable. I knew that meant I'd be gone for a long time.

I felt hurt that my mom wanted to send me away. Was I being punished? Did my mom not want me around anymore? Was I being discarded? Sure, we butted heads a lot, but she was still my mom. No kid wants to believe his mother doesn't love him.

Mrs. Wilfork calmed my fears. She told me I could grow and better myself at the ranch and said this would be a good opportunity for my mom to do the same at home. I didn't understand what that meant. I was still in the dark about how I was conceived, nor did I realize how young my mother was to be raising four boys. But my mother and I weren't getting along, and I knew I wasn't all to blame, so it felt good to hear that we'd both be working on ourselves.

There were still no guarantees I'd get accepted to the Boys Ranch, Mrs. Wilfork told me. The waitlist was long. It could take six to 18 months before enough kids moved out and I could move in.

But Mrs. Wilfork was not someone to sit idly by. She knew my mother and I needed this, and she made some calls, pulled some strings, and maybe twisted some arms. To this day, I don't know what she did or how she did it — and Mrs. Wilfork never did confess — but three weeks after my tour, I was informed that I'd jumped to the front of the line. If I wanted to go, I had to pack my bags right away, I was told, because I needed to be at the ranch in a few days.

My grandmother was the only person I visited before I left. I was so fed up with my hometown, there wasn't anyone or anything I wanted to see one last time. My mom drove me to the ranch. I slept nearly the entire four-hour drive. When we arrived, my mom checked me in at the administration building, gave me one last sobbing hug, and was on her way.

I felt both alone and excited.

The cottage I stayed in was the nicest home I'd ever had. Built of clean red brick, it had five bedrooms — two boys to a room — plus an apartment for the "cottage parents," a married couple who looked after the kids. We had a dining room and kitchen, a game room with a pool table, and a living room with a big TV and comfortable couches. I thought, "This is the life." That is, until I learned about the rules and the schedule.

The ranch is centered around four pillars — work, study, pray, and play — and those four pillars truly guided us and turned the troubled kids into fine adults.

We woke at 7 a.m. Chores like cleaning the bathroom and tidying our rooms and making sure the cottage looked pristine had to be completed by 8:00. We then ate breakfast as a "family," meaning all 10 boys and the cottage parents sat together, said grace, ate, and cleaned up.

Lunch was served in the cafeteria, but dinner was again a family affair, followed by evening chores, which included doing our own laundry when needed.

Table rules during meals included mandatory grace, no overt clowning around, no singing, and no yelling.

The work program provided us campus jobs. We worked an hour every weekday afternoon and four hours on Saturdays.

New kids would start on Cottage Crew, which entailed more advanced chores around their residence — mowing the grass, trimming bushes, washing windows, and whatever basic maintenance work the house needed — and would stay on Cottage Crew for 30 days. Then they were given a job on the actual ranch.

My first job on the ranch was in the auto shop where the campus cars and tractors were maintained. It paid $1.50 an hour. My first duties included unscrewing tires — probably because of my strength — sweeping, mopping, and cleaning the bathrooms, and after eight or nine months at that job, I moved on to replacing tires and assisting the mechanic. To this day, I hate the scent of GOJO soap. I smelled it every day I worked in that garage, and not even a long hot shower with repeated hand scrubbing could wash away the aroma.

At night, following dinner and before evening chores, we had mandatory study hall. If tutoring was needed, it was provided. Grades were checked daily.

The pray pillar was based upon Judeo-Christian beliefs. Chapel was weekly. We did devotion in the homes. Administration made sure religion was part of our everyday dialogue.

As for that fourth pillar — play — I had little opportunity to indulge in that at the beginning.

Like the summer camp, ranch administration did not want to discipline by screaming at us. They explored different ways, though.

Boys at the ranch were ages 10 through 18. The younger half of the kids resided in cottages in "the valley," the area of lower elevation, while the older kids stayed on "the hill," named for obvious reasons. But we had free rein of the campus until we proved that we could not handle it.

The ranch did not want to set the bar low by caging us in just because we were kids who struggled with behavior issues. Instead, they set the bar high and left it up to us to soar higher or sink back into our old routine. They simply told us the rules and expectations, and if we followed them, our world remained big and our privileges grew. For instance, on weekends, the best-behaved kids were taken to sporting events and water parks and got to go fishing and swimming in the nearby springs.

If we misbehaved, however, our world shrunk. If we got into a fight, we were banned from the gym for a week. Trips were off-limits to anyone who was disciplined that week. Early on, I was by far the worst behaved of all the kids at the ranch. I struggled to adjust to being told to follow so many rules.

Nothing about the actual ranch rules bothered me. I had to make my bed back home. I did my own laundry back home. I loved working in the mechanic shop. Since I had no lawn in South Florida, I enjoyed that cottage work. Back home, we ate as a family, and I went to church. I'd have followed all those rules anyway if I had been left to my own devices. But because administrators demanded, I rebelled.

Initially, I wrongly viewed the ranch as an institution. While there may not have been fences and bars and armed guards, I felt like I had been placed inside a system nonetheless. Because I was Black and poor, I had been born into systems: the system of government assistance, the system of low-income housing, the system of going to low-rated schools. I felt that if I was ever arrested, the justice system would not be on my side. As a poor Black male, I thought I'd be forever labeled a criminal. No matter how hard I tried to be a law-abiding citizen, the justice system would never let me forget my mistake. I also felt I'd be less likely to receive fair treatment in court compared to how those from affluent backgrounds are treated.

The education system, the financial system, the justice system — I was on the bottom rung of them all, and I felt there was no way out. Even as a kid who, like all kids, was more engrossed in my singular world than the actual world, I knew what happened to those who got swept up in the system. I knew my history. I learned all about the horrific racial and social inequalities that have persisted. Some, tragically, still go on today in society and were still going on when I first arrived at the Boys Ranch. It filled me with anger and made me feel like the system was working against me.

I've never been motivated by race alone, but it is impossible to turn a blind eye to the reality that no matter how much money I make, no matter how successful I am, no matter how many people I help, there are always going to be bigots who think I am nothing but the N-word. It is a fact that, I now understand, is the racists' deficiency — not mine. But when I arrived at the ranch, I lacked the maturity to deal with the racist world into which I was born. So, I had a "me versus them" attitude.

The town of Live Oak, where the ranch is located, didn't help my attitude. At the time I was there, unofficial segregation remained a rule. At high school football games, the Black fans sat in one section and the whites in another.

The projects where I was raised were predominantly Black, with the minority consisting mostly of Latinx families and a small population of white ones. My schools were mostly Black. Live Oak, however, looked like one of those small towns in movies about Black people who end up in the wrong type of town. To me, it looked like the deep, deep, Deep South. The residents chewed tobacco, dipped, drank beer, and drove around in pickup trucks. I was a minority and was treated as such, but back home, I was among the literal majority most everywhere I frequented.

Being a minority in every way in Live Oak was more of a culture shock than the cows and the manure.

I admit I was wrongly stereotyping, but did I experience blatant racism in Live Oak? Yes — and I'll discuss that later. Did that mean every white person in Live Oak was out to get me? No — but I had a "prove me wrong first" attitude toward everyone.

With all that swimming in my head as a kid, I was not only blind to the good in all people but I was also blind to the good that the ranch offered. "It was part of the system," I wrongly thought, "and I'm going to fight it."

Take the cottage parents, for instance. These men and women were angels. They willingly moved in with 10 troubled boys from different backgrounds and sought to turn them into a family.

They taught kids, some of whom had never had clean clothes to wear or healthy food to eat, how to do their own laundry and how to cook their own meals, they helped with their homework, and they only raised their voices as a last resort.

To the boys, screaming was comfortable. It's what we relied on to express our emotions. The cottage parents understood we weren't so much yelling at them as we were yelling at everyone in our lives who had disrespected us prior to arriving at the ranch. We were just taking our anger out on them.

Instead of disciplining us with anger, they'd want to talk it out and find out why we were truly angry.

Then they'd share such beliefs as, "Integrity is doing what is right even when nobody is looking," so that they could impact us long term.

Most were retired and had already raised children of their own. They were paid, but not much. It was a calling for them, not a paycheck. Such people deserve all the respect in the world, but I started out by showing them none.

To foster a family environment, we were asked to refer to our cottage parents as though they were our parents. My first cottage parents were Mom and Pop Parsley, and that's still how I refer to them today. But when they were first introduced to me, I thought, "There is no way in hell I am calling these two old white people Mom and Pop." I had never met my father, but I sure as hell knew it wasn't that man. And I already had a mom. We may not have always gotten along, but I wasn't going to replace her.

I called them Mr. and Mrs. Parsley, and the more they pushed for me to call them Mom and Pop, the more I rebelled. One thing about me: no one can make me do anything I don't want to do. It wasn't until everyone stopped pressing me to call them Mom and Pop that I finally did so.

Roger Bouchard, who was in charge of the residential care program when I was at the ranch, has since told me that I arrived with a strike against me. From the start, Boys Ranch administration was torn on whether I was a good fit for their system.

There were kids there who had done way worse things to earn a spot at the ranch. But I had a freakish size and strength for someone so young and, according to my record, lacked maturity and respect for authority and was prone to strike out violently. There was concern that I would be a hazard to the administration and to the other boys, and from the moment Mr. Bouchard saw me walk into the cafeteria on my first day, he wondered if they'd made the right decision.

Early on, I did everything I could to let them know they had not. I got into my first fight a week or two after I had arrived. A kid fouled me hard while we were playing basketball at the gym. Two plays later, I fouled him harder. We engaged in a heated argument. He said something about my mom. Boom. Down he went. I was banned from the gym for a week.

I spent my first few days at the cottage without a roommate.

Then Theron, the southern kid I knew from summer camp, moved into my room.

He was my white twin. He didn't look like me, but he was just like me: he liked to push buttons, especially my buttons. The issue was that I could dish it out, but I could not take it. Sometimes, before our morning room inspection, Theron would jump to my side, mess up my bed, toss clothes on my floor, and run back to his side. Then, as I was being disciplined and told to clean my room, he'd stand in the corner and silently chuckle. I was not the type of guy who would rat someone out for something so petty, but my rage built every time he pulled a stunt like that.

One day, I was on edge and in no mood for Theron. As I got dressed, I noticed that my new pack of underwear had been opened and it was missing a pair. I'd just bought that underwear with the money I'd earned working on the ranch.

Furious, I confronted Theron in the cottage living room. With a big cheesy smile on his face, Theron said, "We're roommates, dude. What's yours is mine and what's mine is yours. That's how it works."

"No," I yelled back, along with some expletives. "That's not how this works. I worked for that, not you!"

He made another smart-ass comment, and I went right after him. A few things were knocked over, but there were enough guys from the cottage to pull us apart before it got out of hand. Then Mom and Pop Parsley ended it in the manner they always ended such outbursts — one fish-hooked Theron and one fish-hooked me, pulling us in separate directions.

I remained in that cottage but was moved into a different room. My new roommate was a boy named Tim, the only other Black kid in my cottage. He was really, really skinny and talked with a lisp. I walked into the cottage living room three weeks later and there was good ol' Theron, picking on Tim.

I stood up for Tim and got into another fight with Theron.

At the ranch, a kid was moved to a new cottage if the cottage parents felt that they couldn't get through to him or if they felt he was a danger to the other boys. The hope was that a different cottage parent approach and different assortment of boys would bring about better results. That theory did not work for me.

They moved me to another cottage, but a week later, I got into another fight. I was moved again, fought again, and moved again. I'd arrived in April, and by mid-summer I was already on my fourth cabin.

I never started the confrontations — it was always someone messing with me or me defending someone else. But just like back home, my instinct was to fight. I'd never suggest we talk it out. If someone challenged me to a fight, I fought. If someone thought they could beat my ass, I'd say prove it. Like my mom always said, "Wherever you show out, I'm gonna show out, and it ain't gonna be pretty."

I'd had to fight for everything in life — I didn't know any other way.

Mr. Bouchard has since told me that my name and the trouble I caused were brought up every morning at the daily staff meeting. The female administrators and cottage mothers were the angriest. I at least showed the men some respect, they'd say, but I showed them none. I was not purposely more disrespectful to the women, but I do believe that because of my size, I appeared more intimidating to them than I did to the men.

The administration could handle kids who misbehaved. But when a child was perceived to be a threat to himself, the staff, or the other kids, they had to consider sending him home. One kid was not going to be allowed to hinder the development of the entire ranch. I was that kid.

The administrators tried to get through to me. I'd meet with campus social workers, and they'd explain to me that it's OK to be angry, but it is not OK to be so angry that I cuss people up one side and down the other, and it's not OK to fight. At first I didn't listen to a word they said, and instead endured grueling punishment after grueling punishment. Every time I fought, I had to dig up a tree stump. One was so large that they needed to attach chains to it and haul it away with a tractor.

That gave me an idea.

Next time I got into trouble, they had me dig up a pine tree stump — with a spoon. Administration officials who were there that year laugh and say that's my "walking to school uphill both ways" story, but I swear it happened.

I had used that spoon to dig out a little more than half of that stump when ranch boys drove by on a tractor. I waved them down and convinced them to attach chains to it and pull the rest of the stump from the ground. Man, I loved beating the system.

Another time I was digging up a stump outside the mechanic shop, and Mr. Bouchard pulled up in his car to check on me.

"How much longer do I have to do this?" I asked.

"That's up to you," he replied. "You can work hard and be done today or slack off and be here for days."

Before he drove away, he said one last time, "It's all up to you, Thaddeus."

Knowing all this about my early behavior at the ranch, it should come as no surprise that the administrators who still work there have a nickname for a boy who acts out during his first few months: "Little Thaddeus."

And today, when they can't get through to a "Little Thaddeus," they call Big Thaddeus. I never let the ranch down.

Even in September 2017, when Hurricane Irma was on a path for the Tampa Bay area where I live, I helped when they called. Not knowing how long I'd be gone for if the hurricane hit, I stopped by the ranch before I evacuated with my family. They needed me to talk to a kid they said was extra-hardheaded, though not quite as difficult as I was.

He had a young mother and brothers, but he had been placed into the foster system. He felt like he had been thrown away. He was raising holy hell about wanting to go somewhere else, but he spent a lot of time at the ranch gym, where my photo now hangs, so administration hoped that he'd be willing to hear me out. I told him when I was his age, I was walking in those same shoes, and it was a struggle for me to figure out that these people were here to help me. It was a struggle for me to get on their program, because I was used to doing my own thing.

The kid said to me, "Man, I don't know why they're tripping." I told him he was wrong, they're not tripping, "they're trying to teach you how to be on time, how to be responsible, how to be accountable. Because guess what? When you have a job, and you show up late one too many times, your ass is going to get fired. If you're on a sports team, and they can't trust you to know the plays, to know where to be, and to be there on time, then guess what? You won't be playing much, no matter how great of an athlete you are. And if no one trusts you as a human being, if you lie a lot, if you're unreliable, then you won't get far in life because character counts more than anything else.

"I learned that through hard work and by digging tree stumps and cutting grass and baling hay. They're going to work you because you need to learn how to work. But they're also going to love you in a way that may make you feel uncomfortable at first. When I first got here, I didn't like the fact that I had to call a white woman and a white man Mom and Pop. I didn't like the fact that I had to wake up and make my bed before I did anything else. I didn't like the fact that I had to wash dishes and do laundry on a schedule. But guess what? All that stuff I didn't like made me a better man. And that is what they are doing for you."

Last I heard, that boy is doing well, and not because of me but because he opened himself up to accept all the Boys Ranch has to offer. He has study hall time. He has counselors and cottage parents who communicate with his teachers and the administrators. If he is struggling, those cottage parents and counselors work together to help him find his way. Most importantly, he receives all that assistance in a nurturing environment. That is what we call transformational change.

But since not every kid has access to the Boys Ranch or a school like Academy Prep, we need to work to create more of these kinds of transformational situations.

I don't want to say that public school education is transactional, but I do think many have a transactional method of dealing with children. At too many public schools, they provide students with education but no skills to help them deal with the issues that will prevent them from fulfilling their potential.

Some public schools — especially those that are Title I — embrace transformational methods by providing a free option for kids to stay late after school if they don't have anyone waiting for them at home. Those after school programs offer tutoring and counseling. Some public schools even offer food pantries that their students and their families have access to, so they have dinner and meals on weekends. And some schools even provide clothing to their kids and parents alike. But we still don't have enough schools providing at-risk kids all that they need, putting some students at a disadvantage.

Not all kids from well-to-do backgrounds have what they need to succeed — they go wayward too — but they do have more resources. If these kids lose their way, they can get back on track more easily than those who come from underserved communities. They likely can pay to go to counseling if they are having behavioral issues or hire a tutor if they are struggling in school.

Now look at the less privileged. They can't afford tutoring or counseling for the kids. The parent or parents might have to work so much that they are rarely home, so the kids are on their own. And those parents' jobs are likely not the types of careers that inspire pride in the child or the parent.

So, inspired in large part by the Ron Clark Academy in Atlanta, my ultimate goal is to create my own school that embraces the lessons I have learned from the Boys Ranch and Academy Prep.

If you spend time in a lower-class community, you'll find they have to be creative in everything they do. For example, they lack musical instruments yet have always found ways to be melodious through genres such as rap and step. They don't have many clothes, yet they utilize what they do have in a way that revolutionizes the fashion industry.

Let kids be creative and change the format of the classes to embrace their artistic imagination. Step away from the box public schools find themselves in and find more ways to incorporate art in the curriculum to help kids to better understand subjects such as math and science.

When you tailor a curriculum to fit individual personalities, they can thrive. Then the same kids who thought they were dumb because they struggled in the standard public schools begin to realize their potential and their confidence flourishes. With confidence comes happiness and inner peace rather than anger.

This is how I envision the school that I intend to one day establish, where it is not so much the curriculum that will make my school transformative. It will be those services offered that can change both the students' and parents' lives for the better.

Education is more than just Xs and Os. It is also about Jennys and Joes.

The best football coaches can have the best plays in the playbook, but if they don't have the athletes who can execute, then they either have to change the playbook to accommodate the players they have or change their players to fit the system.

In education we don't have that latter option.

So in those communities where both the children and their parents always seem to be on the bottom rung of society — education, housing, jobs, and so on — we need to shake things up if we are to break the cycle that has gripped those neighborhoods for generations.

Just as at Academy Prep, I'd want to extend school hours to 11 hours a day or more if need be so that they stay away from those situations that revert them back to their old selves. In doing so, those kids can be transformed.

And, for instance, as many schools now do, we'll have uniforms, so no one gets bullied for how they are dressed and so the parents don't have to worry about buying new school clothes so their kid can fit in.

I also want to set up a laundromat near the school. Either kids can do their own laundry or somebody on staff can help do laundry and be there in the morning if, for instance, a child comes to school in their dirty clothes from the day before, for whatever reason.

My school won't be like a magnet or a charter that is placed in a well-to-do area and then busses in the less fortunate kids. I want my school to be in the impoverished community so that the kids and the parents can take full advantage of the other wrap-around services it provides.

I want the school to double as a community building that brings a sense of pride to the area, hosting midnight basketball games and holding arts and crafts classes for the elderly. I want the residents to look at it as "their building."

To truly do what is best for these kids, we also need to look after their parents and grandparents, so there will also be wraparound services that lift them up: vocational and GED training and a food pantry, for example. I want the school to have temporary housing to help those who have lost a home or are going through a rough financial stretch. Kids are affected by their parents' stress, either directly when the parents lash out or indirectly by feeling sympathetic to the plight.

If we don't support the families and help the parents feel better about themselves, their behavior and outlook will influence their kids in a negative manner.

By providing an intricate support system and a pathway to success, the students, their families, and the administration will become a family of sorts, and that in turn can transform their entire community.

Perhaps I didn't accept the Boys Ranch family and method initially, but in time I did. I am the man I am today because of that.

CHAPTER 6

My grandmother died of breast cancer in 1995. I was 18 years old. She resided in hospice in the months leading up to her passing. Visiting a loved one at a facility meant to make their impending death more comfortable is tough. No one wants to accept the eventual loss.

I visited her as often as I could and enjoyed every moment I spent with her. And that was despite her white southern roommate who had dementia but always seemed to remember me. The moment I walked into their room, she'd say to my grandmother, "There's that *N-word* boy of yours." My grandmother never blinked. She'd just lie back and act like she couldn't hear it. I tried to ignore the ignorance too, but it bothered the hell out of me.

Then one day before I left, my grandmother pulled me aside and told me to promise that if she died first, I'd still visit her roommate. "What?" I thought. "You want me to see this nasty racist woman? Are you losing your mind?"

But she was my grandmother, and I'd do anything for her. So, I agreed. My grandmother did die first, and, as promised, I visited her roommate. But she greeted me differently. She stared at me for five seconds and started to ball. She said, "Oh my God, I am so happy I have the chance to see you again."

She explained that she'd spent her life going to church and obeying all of God's commandments, except one: she had been hateful to His people. She then pulled herself up to give me a hug. I had no idea what was going on. This is the same woman who called me the N-word all the time? I was confused, yet I agreed to hug her anyway. She held on tight and told me I was the son she never had.

When I left her room, the nurses told me how happy they were that I was there. The woman had two daughters, but, unable to watch their mother's mind deteriorate, they hadn't visited her in a long time. At that moment, it made sense to me. Jealous of my grandmother and angry with her kids, she lashed out at me.

I never saw her again — she died a few weeks later. But to this day, I remain thankful I visited her; it proved my mantra correct.

When I say there's no such thing as a bad kid, that "kid" can be aged 10, 12, 15, 32, 35, 45, 55, 65. The kid is the individual, the person. I really mean that there is no such thing as a bad person. There are people who make bad decisions or are taught bad things. There are people who make bad observations and come to bad conclusions because they were raised in or live in a damaging environment.

But I believe most people can be rehabilitated if they are removed from the harmful environment or taken away from destructive influences and put into a better situation.

For me, change started with a basketball.

During those rough first few months at the ranch, the basketball court became my refuge. I loved basketball, even more than football. What kid in the 1990s didn't dream of being Michael Jordan? Whether you were white, Black, or brown, as the commercial said, we all wanted to be "like Mike."

With my height and with hands that could already palm a basketball, I dominated pickup games at the Boys Ranch. It was the first time I had experienced athletic triumph and a feeling of superiority. I became addicted to that sensation. Every night during our two hours of free time between study hall and evening chores, I could be found at the ranch basketball court that looked like it was plucked from the set of *Hoosiers*.

As my confidence grew, so did my ability. In nearly no time at all, the awkward kid who sat the bench for the Delray Rocks was in my rearview window. A physical specimen was emerging. I felt like Jordan whenever I was dribbling a basketball. Looking back, maybe I should have felt like Sidney Deane because I'd soon meet my Billy Hoyle — and learn that maybe white men can't jump, but they *can* play.

Our campus director was Pat Monogue, a six-foot-two middle-aged white man who walked campus in the typical work uniform of white collared shirts and khaki pants. I'd quickly learn he was anything but stuffy. He was as much a staple at the gym as I was, playing games of H.O.R.S.E., 21, half-court two-on-two and three-on-three, or running full-court games that were typically back-and-forth-sprint, run-and-gun affairs.

During my fourth or fifth week at the ranch, we played our first game together. I'd seen him there before, but I had never watched him play, so I didn't know if he was any good. Teams were drawn up and it was Mr. Monogue, three scrubs, and me. I was mad. I had an old man and three guys who could barely dribble a bill. We looked destined to lose. And I hate to lose.

Moments into our full-court game of five-on-five, I learned the valuable lesson of judging a book by its cover. It turned out Mr. Monogue was a stud. He used to play for DePaul Catholic School when it dominated its Chicago Catholic Conference. He then played for St. Leo's University, where he became their all-time assist leader. It was while he was at St. Leo's that the team allowed the first Black students on the team. With that type of resume, he was the perfect mentor for me, and it was a role he embraced.

Those who love them know, sports teach people how to work with others to overcome obstacles and how to communicate. Some learn how to lead, some learn how to follow. And because Mr. Monogue was part of that first integrated team at his school, he had first-hand experience working with people from different backgrounds during a potentially tumultuous period. He knew how to use basketball to connect with me.

We dominated that first game we played together — due, in large part, to Mr. Monogue. He wasn't the fastest or most athletic player on the court, but he was by far the smartest and most efficient. He had a beautiful jump shot that he could drain from seemingly any spot on the court that was within reasonable distance of the hoop. What stood out most was his unselfishness. He knew how to get open and get his shot but chose to distribute the ball and make everyone else better. He was like John Stockton (without the short shorts), and I was his Karl Malone.

From that moment on, if there was a game going on, he pressed to be on my team. Watching him play basketball taught me a lot. When people missed shots or had the ball stolen, even though he was ultra-competitive, he never lashed out. He always said things like, "It's OK, it's OK. Come on, come on. Let's go. We got it." I loved being on his team. Even if we were down 10 to 1 in a game that went to 11, I believed that we had a chance. He taught me that it's never over until it's over. It's the same way in life. If you're struggling with your academics, for instance, until the school year ends, you still have a chance to turn it around.

As we forged a bond on the court, he carefully planted seeds for one off the court. While we were playing basketball, he'd bring up my behavioral issues. He was a real positive-reinforcement guy, so he never said anything like, "Get your stuff together or get out," or "You're not going to be here long with that type of behavior."

Instead, he'd ask for my view on what happened. I'd always tell him the truth. If I messed up, I would tell him I messed up. If I felt like a ranch administrator or teacher was picking on me, I would tell him that too. He would usually say something like, "No, they're just being hard on you because they want to see you succeed," and leave it at that. No long lecture, no screaming at me, telling me to grow up. He would say his piece and return to the game.

Today, I meet a lot of older affluent men who want to help me with my work with at-risk kids but are reluctant because they don't think they will be able to relate. They offer me a check, but I tell them I prefer both their money and their time. If they show up in a tailored suit, of course they won't connect with kids dressed from bins from the Goodwill. If they come dressed casually and show a sincere desire to connect with the kids, they will connect.

Be 100 percent honest and transparent. There's nothing wrong with telling the kids, "Look, guys, I don't really know much about what's going on down here, but I want to help." Once you approach the situation with openness and consistency, you will gain more credibility than somebody who comes in and tells the kids how they *will* help them rather than asks them how they *can* help them. If you take that wrong approach, the kids will think, "Who is this dude?" or "Who is this woman?" or "You have an awful lot of ideas for somebody who doesn't know us."

Connect with the kids on their level. If they play basketball, you play basketball, even if you suck. The kids will appreciate that you are willing to make a fool of yourself. It will mean the world to them that you want to be their friend that badly. Some of these boys or girls may have never known an adult who wanted to spend time with them; meeting one who does can change their perspective.

From the moment I met Mr. Monogue, I felt like he was more like a ranch kid than he was like one of the ranch administrators. I felt like he preferred to be on that basketball court with the kids over being in his office, filling out paperwork. I felt like he needed us as much as we needed him, because we kept him young. I had a level of respect for him that I didn't have for anyone else in a position of authority at the ranch, and I believe he had a better understanding of why I was acting out than anyone else did.

I've since learned that Mr. Monogue was my greatest champion when, in those early months, the administrators debated whether I should remain on campus. He'd tell the staff that I was an intelligent young man whose only fault was a lack of impulse control. I'd lash out, he said, but was calm and level-headed once the turmoil passed. He'd tell staff that he thought I was a charismatic, natural-born leader to whom people were drawn. The ranch staff just needed to figure out how to harness my positive attributes and drown out my negatives.

Then came "the incident." Remember Mom and Pop Parsley from my first cottage? By July, they were back in my life. Parents from another cottage had resigned — not because of me, I swear — and to fill the vacancy, parents were shuffled to different cottages. Mom and Pop Parsley were stuck with me once more, and they were not happy. They had informed administration that they would quit if I lashed out just one time while I was under their supervision. It would be either them or me, they told Mr. Monogue.

"The incident" occurred on an open house day for donors. Over 80 percent of the ranch's funding comes from private donors. That is a big reason why our cottages had to be in pristine condition before we left for the day. The entire campus always had to be what the ranch calls "donor ready." At any moment, a potential or current donor could pop by. If they asked for a full tour, they would get one. The administrators would look as though they were failing their mission to groom fine young men if a cottage was gross and unorganized.

Even more important to the donor pool were open houses. Groups of men and women would come to campus, take a tour, and spend time with the boys so that they could see that the ranch's mission was worth supporting. The kids were told in advance to be well-dressed and well-behaved. From a program standpoint, open house days were the absolute worst days to act out.

The morning of this particular open house day, I was asked to sign a contract that made me promise my fighting days were behind me. I suppose they were trying to prevent any potential problems — unfortunately, it didn't work.

I cannot remember what started the fight that day, or who I fought, but I know it was ugly. There were no donors around to see, but that it occurred on such an important day was a major sin. I then made it worse.

The Parsleys both stuck a finger in my mouth and fish-hooked me away. I was riled up — a mix of adrenaline from the fight and anger at Mom and Pop Parsley for another fish hook. I lost my cool, calling them every bad word in the book. In my history of being disrespectful to authority figures, that was near my apex. I meant every word of it too. It was not a crime of passion. I earnestly thought that they had no respect for me, so I wondered why I should have any respect for them.

The Parsleys locked me in an office inside their cottage apartment and stormed over to see Mr. Monogue in the administration building. Mom and Pop Parsley flat out demanded, "That boy has to go. We cannot control him. No one can."

Someone came to get me from the cottage and took me to see Mr. Monogue. There was a mob of ranch staff waiting for me when I arrived at the administration building. They abandoned their peaceful way of dealing with kids and, all at once, began reading me the riot act about having just signed a contract. This was the final straw.

Mr. Monogue quickly came to my aid. "If you guys don't mind," he calmly told the room, "let's take a break." He took me inside his office.

As I sat there in front of his desk, I had flashbacks of the day I tossed the book at my teacher. I had Coach Bump to protect me then. Mr. Monogue liked me, but I didn't expect a suit-and-tie wearing white man to step up for me in the same way a Black pastor and cop who looked after the rough neighborhoods of South Florida had. I was mentally packing my bags and preparing to prove to those who thought I was trash that they were right and to those who thought I had potential, like Coach Bump and Mrs. Wilfork, that they were wrong.

I struggled to maintain eye contact with Mr. Monogue. "The decision has been made to send you home," he said. "What were you thinking? Why are you always getting into trouble?"

It had been on my mind since I was that little kid chastised for fighting bullies and masking my insecurities with jokes and comedy acts. I finally said it. "I don't know. I'm just a bad kid. That's all I've ever been, that's all I know, and that's what everybody expects me to be anyway. I am a bad kid."

He replied with those eight words that have since become my mantra: "There's no such thing as a bad kid."

Confused, I asked him. "What do you mean?"

In a calm voice, he said, "I'm not going to answer that. I feel like you can turn this thing around. I know you will. Eventually, you'll grow into that answer yourself."

He then said, "I'm not going to send you home. It's going to upset a lot of people, but I want you to know that I love you and I believe in you. That's the reason why I'm keeping you here."

I want you to know that I love you and I believe in you. That one sentence changed my life.

Plenty of people had told me they'd loved me before. But he didn't just say he loved me. He told me he believed in me.

No one had ever said that to me. "I love you and I believe in you" instantaneously had an impact on me. Coach Bump or Coach Stevens had never said that. They'd tell me things like, "You can do better," and "We expect more out of you," but I guess I needed to hear someone flat out say they believed in me.

It was a like a switch flipped inside my brain and I finally understood that I needed to change. This man who barely knew me could have replaced me the next day with a new kid who was more receptive to the ranch, but he loved me and believed in me so much, he was willing to battle his staff just to keep me around.

He gave me his phone number and told me to call him whenever I felt anger, confusion, or frustration building up inside me. I did that a lot. We'd usually meet at the gym to shoot hoops while we chatted. If the gym was closed, he'd open it up just for us. Other times, we'd get into his car and take long drives around the campus or town.

It's frustrating for kids when an adult asks them what's wrong and then immediately states, "Well, that's no excuse." When that happened to me, I always thought, "Why the heck are you asking me then? You knew that you were going to hate whatever answer I gave to you."

Mr. Monogue never treated me that way. He truly listened. If my issue was with cottage parents or other adults, he didn't play the kid card and tell me that adults know best. He admitted that he could see my side and that maybe the adults with whom I took issue could have handled the situation differently, but he also reminded me that they had my best interests at heart. He'd remind me that if he was willing to look at things from my viewpoint, I should try seeing things from the cottage parents' perspective too.

If extended to everyday life, that is a lesson that could solve so many problems. We spend too much time trying to tell people why we think we're right and how they're wrong and not enough time listening to the other side of the argument.

Doing so doesn't mean you'll always end up on the same page. You may not even end up in the same library. But if you listen, even when you disagree, at least you will respectfully disagree. And with respect comes civility. Mr. Monogue taught me that lesson.

A few months after "the incident," I decided to tell Mr. Monogue how much I appreciated all he had done for me.

We were playing basketball alone in the gym, when I said, "You know, one day, I am going to be really famous. I'm going to make something of myself."

And he said, "Well, I'll just be happy if you go to college."

"I'll go to college," I retorted with a laugh. "But I'm going to be famous too."

Determined to get his point through to me, he said, "If you go to college, I'll consider you famous. And when you graduate from college, then I'll feel like you made something of yourself."

Not to be outdone, I got the final word in by saying, "Well, I'm definitely going to college, so I'm going to be famous in your eyes. And then I'll graduate and make something of myself. And then I am going to get famous to the rest of the world."

Mr. Monogue died in 1997. He never got to see me graduate or become a celebrity. Today, I continue to work to make him proud.

When I give lectures, I ask audiences to pick up their cellphone and text, "I love you and I believe in you" to a few of their friends and family who they think need to hear those kind words. You can try it now.

I guarantee one will say, "What the hell is going on?" Another will reply, "Are you alright?" Someone else will text you back, "Is something wrong with you?"

Then you'll receive one reply that says, "I needed that. I had a horrible day."

Words can cut a person down. But words can also build a person up.

CHAPTER 7

For kids from certain backgrounds, it can be difficult for them to envision themselves attending college. It is our duty to let them know that they belong there.

If you are told throughout your childhood that you will end up dead or in jail, it is hard to envision any other future for yourself. Kids need to realize that college is a place for them. It's a place where they can have a great time, where they learn and grow, and where they can come out of their shells. By visiting a college campus and seeing young men and women just like themselves thrive in that environment, they realize it is possible for them too. It becomes an attainable goal that they start to strive for.

Maybe they will return to their school following that experience and say, "I'm going to run for student government; I'm going to play sports; I'm going to join Key Club; I'm going to make the honor roll and earn a spot on the National Junior Honor Society. And if I do all of that, I will have a better chance of getting into college — maybe I'll even earn a scholarship."

When one of my best friends, Ricky Sailor, founded a non-profit called Unsigned Preps, which brings talented high school football players, ages 12 to 18, from around the Tampa Bay area and throughout the state of Florida, on four-day, five-night summer bus tours of college campuses, I signed right up. We run tours of colleges in Florida, Georgia, Mississippi, and Kentucky, visiting at least four different schools in each state. Overall, 27 schools in the southeast region have joined our program, including the University of Florida, Florida State University, University of Mississippi, and University of Alabama.

These young athletes stay in a hotel each night. They get to see every corner of the campus while bonding with other athletes, coaches, and recruiters. Some of the kids who take these tours are highly rated athletes who use this opportunity as their first step toward an athletic scholarship. Others may have what it takes to be highly recruited but do not have the appropriate college mindset. They don't think that college is a realistic goal, so they don't work as hard as they should at improving their game or their grades. Some think talent alone is enough. But I've seen kids from so many walks of life transform during a tour.

They start each week with little knowledge of what it takes to go to college. Then we give them the opportunity to run out of a tunnel and into an arena or stadium and envision themselves doing that during a real game every week. We give them the opportunity to play against their athletic counterparts so that they can understand innate athletic ability is not enough. They realize there are other kids out there who are just as talented, just as big, and just as fast, sometimes more so. If they are going to rise to the top of that class of athletes, they learn quickly that it will take hard work and determination. We then drill into their heads that even if they become the best athlete, they still need good grades because a college will not provide a scholarship to a young athlete who is barely passing high school.

One way we get through to them is by introducing them to college athletes on each campus. Those college players let them know that if a college is choosing between one of them and another high school athlete who has equal ability, it could very well come down to their academics and their character. The school will prefer a player that they are confident can be molded into a leader on and off the field.

What's more, a player of lesser ability may be higher on a recruiter's list than a top tier player if the former's character and grades are highly impressive.

We, as parents, mentors, and coaches, can scream that message until we are blue in the face, yet the teenage players might not hear a word of it. But if they hear it from someone who just recently went through the recruiting process, it registers.

Those same kids who started the week without an understanding of what it takes to achieve a college dream are soon asking me about the ACT and SATs.

My friend Ricky founded the non-profit in 2010. Since then, as I write these words in 2019, the tours have helped obtain athletic scholarships for hundreds of students, some of whom have gone on to the NFL: Ray-Ray McCloud, Ramik Wilson, Joey Ivie, Deon Cain, and Bruce Hector are just a few.

On my own, I offer services for all students, not just athletes. Throughout the year, I load boys and girls from throughout the Tampa Bay area onto buses and take them to Florida colleges and universities. They tour the campuses and talk with first-generation scholarship students who came from similar backgrounds. Many of those first-generation college students were part of one of my tours just years earlier. It means a lot for at-risk kids to meet soon-to-be college graduates who can relate to growing up in a home with an abusive father or going to bed hungry more nights than not. Those kids see themselves in that college student and then envision themselves on that campus.

When kids get the itch to go to college and when

someone proves to them it is a possibility, they will work to get there.

As Ricky Sailor says, "If you let them see it, they will believe it."

Mr. Monogue knew that to be true, which is why he sought to surround me with roommates who could fuel that desire in me. Following "the incident," I changed cottages yet again, this time moving to The Hill where the older ranch boys resided. My new home was Blackburn Cottage. Blackburn had cottage parents who were considered among the best — Mr. and Mrs. Davis.

In my opinion, they were the best at getting through to me.

Mr. Davis was a Navy veteran who ran a construction contracting business in St. Petersburg before he found his next calling as a mentor for troubled kids. Mrs. Davis was as structured as her military husband. She kept a strict schedule from which we were not allowed to deviate for even a moment. During study hall, for instance, if we had no school work to do, she'd assign us an essay rather than allow us to have added free time. The busier we were doing positive things, the less time we had to get into trouble, she figured. As the old saying goes, "Idle hands are the devil's workshop."

The other reason Mr. Monogue thought Blackburn was the best fit for me was because its residents were 17 and 18 years old.

I dwarfed my roommates at past cottages. Mr. Monogue rationalized I would be less likely to lash out against kids my own size. He was right about that. My roommate was Willie Nickerson, a six-foot-two 17-year-old Black kid who was jacked to the gills. He swam and wrestled for Suwannee High School, where the ranch kids attended. He didn't so much succeed in sports because of athleticism but rather because he was just so much stronger than anyone else. Of course, I tested him. I'd challenge him to an amateur wrestling match, and he'd dump me on my head, I'd get up, and he'd dump me again, and so on. I'd go after him until he tapped out from exhaustion even though I never once dominated him physically.

I never tried to fight him in earnest, though, and not because I was afraid. From the start, I looked up to Willie like a big brother. And that was the main reason Mr. Monogue placed me in that cottage. He hoped I'd benefit from living with role models.

Early on, Willie shared his backstory with me. He too was from the South Florida area — Fort Pierce. In middle school, a couple of Willie's friends were hanging out at an arcade. When a car drove by, the driver was identified as someone who'd slept with Willie's friend's girlfriend. That friend chased after the car and tossed a bottle through its back window. The driver jumped from the car and brandished a weapon. Willie's friend ran but was not fast enough. He took a few deadly bullets to the back.

Willie was not there, but he could have easily been at that arcade or in that car with the gunman. When he heard what happened, he realized it was only a matter of time before he was present for a gun fight. Looking for a way out of his neighborhood, he learned about the Boys Ranch and sought out a way to get there. He was determined to make something of himself from the moment he stepped foot on the ranch, he said.

Willie was the cottage's "orientation guy," the resident with whom the new kids stayed because it was known he'd be a good influence. He introduced himself not just by name, but career path. His name was Willie Nickerson, he told me, and he would be going into the military and then law enforcement.

I laughed. Boys Ranch kids don't become the police. But it was no joke. Today, he is a veteran and works in law enforcement.

All the cottage residents introduced themselves in a similar manner.

Jeremy Goodrich, also 17, but white and around five-foot-ten and 205 pounds, wanted to be a veterinarian, for example.

Willie made it very clear: "We do things differently around here. We respect our cottage. We respect each other. We respect one another's property. We do our chores. We work hard. We all want to be something. And if they didn't think you could be something, you wouldn't still be here. Most importantly, we respect Mom and Pop Davis."

Mom and Pop Davis owned a home with a stocked pond a few hours' drive away. On weekends, they'd take those who had behaved during the week there to fish or for a picnic. The older boys were of course not getting into trouble, and not wanting to be the only one left behind, I stayed in line at all times. Mr. Monogue's cabin theory was working.

My new roommates' drive was rubbing off on me too. I'd grab the basketball and yell out to see if anyone wanted to play. Willie would often pull his nose out of his book and sternly say something like, "No, man, I have a calculus test. Don't you have a test?" If I said no, he'd shake his head and reply, "Maybe not tomorrow, but everything you are learning will be on a test at some point."

He was more concerned with trying to make something of himself than trying to bully kids, clown around, or prove that he was King Kong. He knew that because of his background as a poor Black inner-city kid, he had to work twice as hard as other kids. He never complained. If that is what it would take to make it, he said, then he would do it.

Having the older kids around helped my studies too. Some excelled in math. Others English, or history, or science. They all leaned on one another during study hall. Since my lessons were juvenile compared to what they were doing, my cottage-mates could walk me through any academic troubles.

Willie and I grew especially close during the holidays. Most of the other kids went home. Our families and ranch administrators felt that it was best if we remained at the ranch rather than return to neighborhoods that offered nothing but trouble. During those breaks from school, we played a lot of basketball — which I dominated — and ping-pong — his strength.

What I envied most of all was Willie's drive. I was more athletic than he was, but he pushed himself harder than anyone I'd ever met. He was pushing 315 pounds on the bench press — best on campus. We were each in that gym every day, and my goal was to beat his mark. Eventually I did, but because he'd already graduated by then, he says it doesn't count. Well, Willie, I know you are reading this, and I say it counts. If you have an issue with that, we can go to the gym right now and settle it once and for all . . .

By the end of that year, we were working together on the farm. I artificially inseminated my first cow with him. Yeah, you read that right.

When Willie earned his license to drive the tractors, we'd drive the ranch to pick up the raked piles of pine needles and deliver them to the campus dump. In between stops, I'd lay in the wagon on top of a bed of needles. One day we hit a bump, the wagon dislodged, and, unaware, he kept driving. I said nothing. Instead, I lay back and took a nap. He got all the way to the dump before he realized he no longer had the wagon.

He tracked me down, found me napping, and angrily asked why I didn't scream for him. "Shh," I said. "I'm sleeping, man." And he broke down laughing. I then told him, "You have to start using your head, man. You were mad I was sound asleep. But remember, the longer we are out here, the more we get paid." I like to think I had a positive impact on him too. He was so serious, but I showed him how to have some fun.

I'd wake Willie by tickling his ear with a long piece of grass that he'd mistake for a bug every time. Or if he didn't want to get out of bed to go to the gym, I'd dance around the room, making noise to wake him up. Initially annoyed, he'd take a deep breath and remind himself that though I was his size, I was still just a kid. In time, he enjoyed my comedic outbursts.

Things were going so well for me at the ranch that even Theron and I established a positive relationship. We finally realized that rather than fighting each other, we might as well raise hell together. We didn't do anything illegal, just good-spirited teenage pranks.

Take Mom Parsley, for instance. She wore a hearing aid, so one day I stood in front of her and mouthed words but said nothing. She kept asking, "Huh? What did you say?" She then turned up her hearing aid and I began saying a word every few seconds so that it sounded like my sentences were broken up. So she turned up her hearing aid to the max, and Theron went running up behind her and yelled, "Thaddeus!" as loud as he could. I swear she almost hit her head on the ceiling because she jumped so high. By that time, I had made amends with even Mom Parsley, so she was a good sport and laughed with us.

Still, teachers weren't big fans of my sense of humor. I was doing the same things at Suwannee High that bothered my teachers back home. I'd wait until the bell rang and then 30 seconds later burst into class for a grand entrance. During class, I kept making inappropriate jokes at inappropriate times.

But one day, the bell rang, I waited 30 seconds, pulled on the door, and it was locked. I knocked, and the teacher motioned for me to go to the office. Later that week, it happened at another class. Then another. I finally asked the principal what was going on. It turned out a teacher, Ms. Roy, conspired in the joint effort to get me in line. What made that so crazy to me was that I wasn't in any of her classes.

I approached her and asked what was going on. Why did she care what I did? None of it was affecting her. She told me I was wrong. Everything I did affected others. Kids looked up to me, she explained. I had a larger-than-life-personality, I was friendly and athletic. Whether I liked it or not, I was a leader. Other kids wanted to be like me, she said, so I needed to be the best me.

"You have a very bright future, but ability alone is not enough. Being a good athlete or having an outgoing personality or being the smartest kid in school can make you a leader, but that doesn't make you a good leader. You need to learn to harness your leadership abilities and do the right thing. There is no glory in leading a group of losers."

I promised her I'd do better.

I'd still wait outside my classroom until that bell rang. But rather than staying outside another 30 seconds, as I saw the door closing, I'd stop it with my foot and slip inside just in time.

I was still a class clown, and I always will be. But I realized there is a time and place for jokes. Flicking staples is never appropriate. Burping when the teacher is educating the class is never appropriate. Although bothering the class during a test is never appropriate, I learned teachers don't mind if a student brings a little levity to their day — some even appreciate it — but it has to be on their time, not yours.

But, without a doubt, next to Mr. Monogue, no one had as big an impact on my childhood as Charles Blalock.

Mr. Blalock was a civil rights icon in Live Oak. He was the first African American principal in the history of Hamilton County, which neighbored Suwannee. He went on to become the first African American elected as superintendent in Suwannee County and was later elected the first African American superintendent in Hamilton County.

We met before "the incident," when he was the superintendent in Suwannee County. My gym teacher, who saw athletic potential in me but was worried that without guidance I'd be expelled from school, had reached out to Mr. Blalock.

Mr. Blalock was known as more than a superintendent. Like Coach Bump, if he knew a kid needed a straight talk, he'd provide it. If they were lost, he'd help them find their way. I was eating lunch in the cafeteria when my gym teacher introduced me to Mr. Blalock.

"Let's take a walk," the gym teacher told me. "I want you two to talk."

As we strolled the campus, my gym teacher silently peeled himself away, leaving just Mr. Blalock and me. Mr. Blalock then stopped me and demanded, "You think you can whup me?"

"What do you mean?" I asked, terrified. Mr. Blalock — a six-foot-three, 250-pound Black man in a position of power in a white town — was challenging me.

"I asked, 'Do you think you can beat me in a fight?' I think that was pretty clear," he said.

"No," I said.

And before I could murmur another word, Mr. Blalock snapped back, "Because I will fight you."

I remained silent. I had no idea what was going on. I didn't know how to respond. "Here's the deal," he said. "I hear you like to fight. I hear you are not afraid to get into fights. But remember this — there is always someone bigger, badder, madder, and faster than you. If you keep walking around with the attitude you have, sooner or later, you're going to anger the wrong person and the end result might not be positive for you.

"So I will make you a promise. If I hear about you getting into fights, I am going to come back to this school and teach you a lesson before the wrong person does.

"But if you do the right thing, I will be here whenever you need me. I promise."

He lived up to that promise.

Mr. Blalock would stop by the school every so often to check in on me, give me another lecture, and monitor my grades.

A few weeks after "the incident," our true bond was formed. You couldn't just sign up to play sports at the Suwannee High School. The ranch administration first had to assess the boy's maturity and ability to handle the schedule. We still had to participate in daily study halls, and instead of performing work duties right after school, we had to work double duty on Saturdays. We didn't have to miss practice or games, but we couldn't use it as an excuse to blow off our responsibilities. I had done nothing since I'd arrived to prove I could be held accountable for anything.

I had almost been kicked off the ranch in July. Not soon after, football tryouts started. Mr. Monogue gave me a chance anyway.

He knew I loved sports and hoped that being on the team would provide me further incentive to excel in school out of fear of failing and having to quit. Football would also give me a structured environment to let out my aggression. Plus, he figured even less free time meant even less of an opportunity to find trouble. Most importantly, he thought that succeeding on the field would foster the leadership qualities he was certain I had.

Making Suwannee's team was not going to be easy. They'd just come off winning four straight state championships. The Suwannee kids were different than the kids I played with back home. My teammates on the Delray Rocks were far better athletes, but those Suwannee players had a superior work ethic and focus.

A lot of the small-town kids playing for Suwannee grew up working or living on farms. They woke with the roosters to start their work day, went to school, and then worked again until it became too dark to see. The ranch was seeking to instill that same mentality in me, but the Suwannee boys grew up with it. I finally realized why those small-town teams could beat the inner-city teams, even though the city players could wear jeans and flip-flops and still outrun country kids in athletic gear. The country boys had the discipline needed to win.

Still, due to my athletic ability and size, I held my own. I made the varsity team as a freshman. One of the other players on the team was Mr. Blalock's son, Chuck, who was a senior.

Being a great dad, Mr. Blalock rarely missed a practice. And, as promised, he looked after me.

Before preseason was over, Mr. Blalock had unofficially adopted me into his family. After practice, he'd take me back to his house to have dinner with his family. When he took his kids to the movies, he'd invite me.

Sometimes, he'd take me shopping with the family.

Mr. Blalock was a proud alumnus of Florida A&M University, one of the nation's historic predominantly Black colleges. And he hated Florida State University. When he attended FAMU, FSU had not yet been integrated. FAMU students were bullied if they dared take one step onto FSU campus. Still, I grew up watching FSU football and basketball on TV back home. So when we were at a sports store and he asked if I wanted anything, I pointed to an FSU hat.

His kids took a step back. I was unaware of the scorn he had for FSU, but his children knew. Without saying a word about his history with the school, he bought me that hat anyway. Anyone who understands college rivalries and racial history understands that that gesture shows how much he loved me. He did not want to let me down and didn't have the heart to destroy my love for FSU. He did not bend when it came to modern race relations, though.

On one occasion, someone offered him a campaign contribution but asked that he take it in secret. "I believe in everything you're doing and you're a good man," the would-be contributor said. "I want to see you do well. I just ask that you don't let anyone know where it came from."

He looked at the person and righteously said, "I appreciate it. Thanks, but no thanks. If you can't publicly support me, I don't think privately supporting me helps the cause."

The biggest impact Mr. Blalock had on me was seeing how well everyone treated him, even the rich white people, and how he always let them know he was their equal in every way. Mr. Blalock estimated the Black vote in Suwannee County likely made up 10 to 15 percent of the total election, yet he defeated white candidates in elections.

Through him, I learned that Black men could achieve anything and be rightfully seen as equal to whites.

The first time I ever saw a college campus was also with Mr. Blalock. We went to FAMU homecoming weekend just a few months after we first met. There, I saw educated Black men and women studying. I watched one of the greatest marching bands in the world — the FAMU Rattlers band, the Marching 100. Mr. Blalock even took me into the football team's locker room.

What stuck with me was the fun I witnessed — the tailgating, the on-campus comradery, the fraternities. That inspired me to work harder in school and on the football field so that I could one day go to college and have that experience. When the weekend was over, I told Mr. Blalock, "I would love to go to college here."

To my surprise, he said, "Don't. Why would you eat hamburger when you could eat steak?"

"What do you mean?"

"Would you rather be on a bus for eight hours, play a game, get right back on the bus, eat snacks, and go to class the next day sore? Or would you rather ride in a plane, get to your away game in two hours, stay in a nice hotel, get the best medical attention so your body can recover, and then fly home in comfort? Look, FAMU is my alma mater, and I love it. But you have the potential to be one of the best players in the nation. I believe that. You can dine on steak. Reach for that goal."

When his son, Chuck, graduated high school at the end of my freshman year, I moved into Mr. Blalock's home on weekends. He'd pick me up at the ranch nearly every Friday, and he'd bring me back Sunday nights. During weekends, we did father-son activities

— watch movies, go fishing, and attend college games at all the Florida universities and colleges.

One weekend, following a trip to watch a college football game, we were back at his house late, wired from the excitement of the game. We were still awake at around 1 a.m., chatting about life, when I finally asked what had been on my mind since we bonded. "Mr. Blalock," I asked, "do you mind if I call you Dad?"

I meant it. He was everything I thought a dad should be.

"On one condition," he replied. "Only if I can call you Son."

He still calls me his son today.

I will forever love Mr. Monogue and always consider him one of my greatest mentors, but I truly needed a strong Black male role model in my life. Mr. Blalock became that man for me. He was a father figure, a leader of men and women, an unapologetic lover of people, and a speaker of truths. Mr. Blalock didn't need another young man in his life. He had a son, plus two daughters, Tracy and Carla. He took on the added responsibility anyway. He was someone I wanted to make proud.

A few years ago, when Mr. Blalock was in Tampa for a visit, he attended a talk I gave to a group of at-risk kids. As he tells it, he was at first taken aback by the crowd of kids excitedly calling me Titus and asking for my autograph.

Then, he said, he listened to the words I spoke and heard a lot of what he had told me when I was in their same position.

That trip to FAMU is what inspired the college campus tours I now host. But that's far from the only thing I borrowed from Mr. Blalock. When I meet a kid who, like childhood me, is prone to getting into fights, I conjure up my inner Mr. Blalock and ask if he thinks he can beat me in a fight. That always ends the same way it did when Mr. Blalock challenged me. Their bravado disappears and, in its place, there is a humble kid willing to listen to what I have to say.

Let's be clear: I would never lay a hand on a child and nor would Mr. Blalock.

Just as Mr. Blalock did with me, my promise to take them on in a fight is always joined by my belief that they can be a better version of themselves. I promise them that I will do whatever it takes to help them overcome whatever obstacles are negatively impacting their lives. My wording makes it clear that I in no way want to fight them. I instead want to help them.

The challenge is a way of reminding them that there is always someone bigger and badder than them out there, and, unlike me, that person might not have their best interests at heart. It's difficult for me to explain, though, how to know which kids will respond positively to that approach and which will be pushed further away.

I go with my gut.

I look for those kids who remind me of myself at their age.

I am not just the product of Mr. Blalock's example, though. I often find myself also mimicking Coach Bump, Coach Stephens, the Wilforks, Ms. Roy, and, of course, Mr. Monogue. It truly takes a village.

So many people helped shape me into the man I am today. In return, I am compelled to pass their wisdom on to others.

CHAPTER 8

Is it any surprise that Thanksgiving is one of my favorite days of the year?

With an appetite like mine, how could I not look forward to a giant serving of perfectly roasted, fried, or smoked turkey? Hell, I'd take a serving of all three on the same plate and then surround it all with an assortment of sides, especially some green bean casserole.

Not only do I cook my own Thanksgiving meal, I sometimes go meal hopping, visiting my friends' homes and tasting what they've prepared. I love the variety.

But I promise, even on such a food lover's holiday, my heart remains larger than my stomach.

In April 2018, a Tampa Bay high school pitcher named Alec Barklage was complaining about pain in his leg. Alec thought he tore something while running sprints at practice. A trip to the hospital told him otherwise — he had a broken fibula that was caused by bone cancer. It was discovered by the grace of God. If he hadn't broken his lower leg in that place and at that time, the cancer may have gone undiscovered for much longer, spread to his entire body, and been impossible to cure.

Alec had a four-inch tumor removed and underwent massive amounts of chemo.

A few months later, his neighbor and my friend, Rob Elder, told me what Alec had had to overcome and that he was a WWE fan. So I sent him a video reminding him that if he stayed strong, stayed positive, and put his faith in God, he would win this fight and become a role model to others who face the same adversity. I was supposed to have lunch with him a short time after I sent the video, but he was too ill to meet, so it was cancelled. Then, the night before Thanksgiving 2018, my friend Rob gave me an update on Alec's health.

He had had his ups and downs, but at that moment the chemo had him in a bad way. Rob was on my scheduled Thanksgiving dinner tour, and he hoped that I could also take a moment to meet with Alec. Perhaps a visit from a WWE Superstar could make this particular Thanksgiving all the more memorable for him.

Of course I'd be there, I said. I won't lie, Rob also promised me one heck of a meal, and he came through, but the true joy of that day was seeing Alec smile. He was so appreciative of the time we spent together. I reiterated to him that day that I knew he would beat the cancer and that God had a plan to use him to bring joy to others. He promised he'd come through. God did his part. Alec is cancer free.

My philanthropic resume is proof of my dedication to helping those in need and paying it forward. By appearing at events or volunteering as a spokesman for non-profits, I have helped to raise millions of dollars for charities. I have also mentored countless kids, assisted high schoolers in securing athletic and academic scholarships, and made sure tens of thousands of the less fortunate kids and families who wake up to so little during the holiday season receive something special.

No matter where my travels may take me, whether it is for a WWE live event or a visit with friends, I always try to fulfill WWE's mission, "Put smiles on faces," whether it's by taking pictures with fans or through an inspirational speech to a youth group.

I enjoy every aspect of being able to change people's lives, and I always have. I have used my platforms as a high school All-American and University of Florida Gator and now as a WWE Superstar to constantly, continuously, and consistently work to better the lives of others. There is no question that being a WWE Superstar and having the celebrity that comes with it could be a blessing or a curse. I choose to use it as a blessing to help countless families around the world.

There are well over 100 WWE Superstars on the main roster, and I am proud that we all share the same mission — to put smiles on faces both as entertainers and as philanthropists. We all have our own stories and, because of those differences, as a unit we can relate to people from every corner of this world and utilize our platforms to bring them joy. We all do our part.

Still, no one is obligated to give back. No one should feel like they are forced to help others. Philanthropy is an honor and a privilege, not a burden. If you don't want to help others, don't. But I believe that everyone inherently wants to be charitable, they just need to find their inspiration.

Some, for instance, give back because of a life experience. I know Alec will use the strength and determination he used to beat cancer to now inspire others who are trying to do the same. My philanthropic motivation came toward the end of my junior year of high school. It was then that my mother decided it was time to tell me the truth.

I was doing well. My behavior had improved, I was making honor roll, and I was first team all-state in football, second team all-state in basketball, and all-conference in track. Still, my relationship with my mother remained strained. We talked regularly. She knew I'd turned my life around. She told me how proud of me she was. But there remained a barrier between us.

My mother believed that telling me about the circumstance of my conception could break that wall. It was not an easy decision for her to make. She admits she was scared. Rape victims live with a sense of shame, even though they did nothing wrong. It's hard for them to discuss the rape with counselors, let alone tell their teenage son. She was also worried about how I would react. I had come so far. Would hearing the tale reignite my rage and send me into a downward spiral?

She spoke with her counselor, and then she spoke with the ranch counselors. All agreed that if she wanted to tell me about my conception that it was as good a time as any. I was working on the farm, artificially inseminating cows — yep, you read that right again — when an administrator told me that I was needed in the main office immediately.

I didn't know what was going on, but I figured it was important. My mom had arrived a few hours earlier to meet with the counselors and discuss all the possible outcomes of telling me. In the worst-case scenario, they worried I'd get violent, so the counselors let her know that they had to be in the room to help calm me if it played out in such a manner.

I was escorted into a conference room where two counselors plus Mr. Monogue, my cottage parents, and my mom were seated. I was not expecting her, so I was immediately nervous.

Before my mom spoke, the counselors put my mind at ease by saying I was not in trouble, and I was not being sent home. Then the small talk started. How was school going? She hoped to watch me play football. My brothers were doing fine and were proud of me too.

Then she brought up Charles, the man from my early childhood who pretended to be my father. He's not your dad, she said. In my mind, I laughed. I knew that as a little kid, and it became more obvious as I grew older and larger. He stood maybe five-foot-seven and weighed 150 pounds. There was no way his genetics coursed through my body.

I told my mom I knew Charles wasn't my dad. I'd always known, I said.

And then she just blurted it out. She was raped when she was 11, she said. I was the product.

First, I was shocked. Next, I cried for a bit. When I regained my composure, I asked if she knew who did it, and she told me the terrible details.

"Do you know where he's at?" I asked.

"No," she said. "But I know his name, and I think he's still around that area. I can probably find him if you want to meet him."

What more do you need to know about my mother? If I wanted to know my father, a man who raped her, she was willing to set it up. She's the most loving parent a son could want.

I told her I had no desire to meet him. To this day, that sentiment remains true.

At that moment in that conference room, any hate I'd ever harbored for my mother instantly turned to love. I had an entirely different perspective on everything. I apologized to her for everything bad I'd ever done, for every disrespectful thing I'd ever said to her, and for making her life even more difficult. I finally saw the mom of my childhood for who she was: a kid — a scared and confused kid raising a scared and confused kid.

She gave up her childhood so that she could bring me into this world. She never had the opportunity to become a cheerleader, go to prom, nervously hold hands with a boy on their first date, go to the mall with friends, or walk across the stage on graduation day. She lost those innocent years of her life so that she could give me life. She gave up everything so that she could give me everything.

From that day on, my mother and I have been as close as a mom and son should be. That wall between us was shattered. We talked often prior to that, but we never really talked. I shared what was going on in my life, but I didn't share what was going on in my head or heart. That changed, and she became a bigger part of my life. I'd never invited her to come to any of my football games before that day, but I invited her to all my games after that. It meant the world to me knowing that my mom was in the stands, watching her son, who once sat the bench for the Delray Rocks, grow up to be a high school star athlete. Seeing her proud of me filled me with joy.

I won't denigrate anyone who is pro-choice or, for their own personal reason, decides to have an abortion. I do not judge.

I was brought into this world under unfortunate circumstances. For mothers who were impregnated under similar circumstances, I see both sides of the argument over whether to have the child or not.

On one side, someone was raped. She did not ask to have a child, and that kid was conceived out of anger and violence, not love. On the other side, if she decides to have the kid, she has the opportunity to raise that child to become someone who turns the negativity of the conception into a positive for the world. Or, if a mother does not think she can raise that child properly, she can find someone who can. There are people out there who have the means yet cannot conceive. Many are looking for children to adopt.

Ever since that day when my mom told me the truth, I felt an added burden — a burden I welcomed.

"'For I know the plans I have for you,' declares the

Lord, 'plans to prosper you and not to harm you, plans to give you hope and a future.'" — Jeremiah 29:11

Up to that point, I had been trying to prove people wrong. I'd been told I'd be dead or in jail by the time I was a teen, and I was focusing on shutting those people up.

But when I learned the truth about my conception, my goal changed. It was no longer to prove people wrong; instead, I wanted to prove that my mother and God were right to give me life. God makes a message out of every mess and a testimonial out of every test.

I left that meeting knowing that I was there because God had a purpose for me.

I started piecing together everything about my life.

I'd never gone to jail, even though I may have deserved some time in juvenile detention. I'd never been shot, even though I grew up in an environment where that was a possible scenario.

I thought about how I'd jumped to the front of the line to get into the Boys Ranch and wondered what would have happened if I'd remained in Boynton Beach longer — perhaps something terrible would have happened to me, or maybe I would have done something terrible.

I thought about how Coach Bump had saved me, how Mr. Monogue had given me more chances than I'd deserved, how Mr. Blalock had taken me under his wing, and how Ms. Roy, who didn't even have me as a student, had decided to go out of her way to teach me a positive lesson.

Why did I deserve so many chances? Why did so many people look out for me? What had I done right? The only answer I could come up with was that God had a plan for me.

I sat alone in my bedroom that night and told myself I would become one of the best high school football players in the country, I would go to college, I would be a collegiate football player, and I would graduate. Then, rather than using those successes to benefit only myself, I would become a role model. I would tell my story and teach kids that if I could rise from the ghetto, they could too.

Shortly after my mom revealed the truth about my conception, I confided in Mr. Blalock that if I ever met the man who raped her, I might kill him. He calmly shook his head and told me, "Son, that is no way to live your life. Don't be vengeful. Don't be angry. Forgive. Use your life to inspire others."

That's what I'm doing.

CHAPTER 9

I bleed University of Florida orange and blue. Want to know how much?

Let me walk you through a scenario.

There are just seconds to go in the fourth quarter of the College Football Playoff National Championship game between the University of Florida and arch rival Florida State University. University of Florida is winning by six, but FSU has the ball at the goal line. If the FSU quarterback passes the ball to an open wide receiver in the end zone, and that wide receiver is my son, you better believe I'll be praying he drops the ball. I would root against my own kid.

Does that make me a terrible dad? Nope. He could have gone to the University of Florida and competed for a national title while walking the hallways of the greatest college in all the world.

My sons are stud athletes. That's not a dad bragging. That's a fact. They are first-class athletes. But, more importantly, they are first-class students and people.

With such qualities, I feel certain they will have their choice of colleges.

If two of those options are Florida and FSU, do I think they'll choose the latter? I'm not sure. They grew up on the University of Florida sidelines, and while I'm confident that they would pick my alma mater, I wouldn't pressure them to pick the Gators over the Seminoles. But I'll cheer for only one team. They know which one that is.

My primary advice to my sons and all high school athletes is that when picking a college, do what is best for you.

Do not choose a school because your mom or dad went there. Do not choose a school because your brother or sister was a big star there. Do not choose a school because people expect you to go there.

No one in the athlete's family nor any of their friends will be going to practice. None of them are going to work with the coaches. None of them are going to sweat through two-a-days. None of them will be staying up late to finish papers or cram for finals. None of them are going to spend the next four years of their life on that campus. They will be there on game days, a few weekend visits a year, and graduation. That's it.

My advice to parents with children who are star recruits: do not pressure your child to go to your first-choice school. That's selfish.

A student athlete needs to go somewhere that they feel provides them with the best opportunity to succeed both in the classroom and athletically. They need to go to the school that will provide them with the most opportunities to help them become the best version of themselves and will give them the skills to keep improving upon that version.

I originally thought my best athletic opportunity was on the basketball court. Then Suwannee High School's varsity football coach Mike Pittman told me otherwise.

Always on the lookout for a future star, he often attended local competitions that featured seventh and eighth grade standout athletes. He could be found everywhere a game was being played and did not discriminate against any sport. Coach Pittman attended peewee football, little league baseball, recreational soccer, wrestling matches, and so on. And if he saw a potential football star, he let that kid know, in no uncertain terms, that he expected to see him at varsity tryouts someday.

Since I was only there for the last few months of middle school, I didn't play any organized sports, but I was killing it in gym class. Whatever sport we played, I dominated. Coach Pittman was at my gym class just days after the gym teacher let him know about the new eighth grade star athlete who was already the size of a man.

I had a pair of those safety goggle–like eye glasses that James Worthy, the Los Angeles Lakers forward from the 1980s, made famous. I wore them everywhere. They were much cooler than the quad-focals. And the first thing Coach Pittman asked me was if I thought I was James Worthy.

"Well, sir," I said, "I am a basketball player."

"Young man," he replied in his country accent, "you're also fixing to play football for me, and I don't wanna hear no argument. You might like basketball, but that ain't gonna be your meal ticket. Football — that is your meal ticket."

How could I say no to that?

As I mentioned earlier, I was good my freshman year. It can be hard for a kid that young to stand out against kids who are going to be naturally stronger and faster simply due to age, but I earned myself regular playing time that season.

Then, during my sophomore season, I earned a starting spot as defensive tackle and was selected third team all-county. It was during that sophomore year that recruiters let me know an athletic scholarship was possible. At first, I'd receive around five to six letters a week from smaller schools, like

Furman University, South Carolina University, and Mississippi State University. By the end of that school year, the count jumped to 10 a week, and by the beginning of my junior year, it amped up to 15, 20, 25, and sometimes 30 a week. By the time that season was over, I was getting as many as 100 a week. The phone calls were just as rampant — every night, three to five recruiters would check in with me. They'd call my coach too.

Junior year had been my real breakout season. Though the teenage me wouldn't have admitted it, I have to give Coach Pittman credit for turning me into a sought-after player. My athleticism — my strength and my speed — was due to my God-given genetics. The football knowledge came in large part from Coach Pittman.

Coach Mike Pittman picked on me early on. I'm confident he did so because I was from the Boys Ranch. That he thought he had to be tougher on the kids perceived as undisciplined. The only other ranch boy on the team was J.W. Harden, also Black and from the inner city; he was picked on too, adding to my belief.

In one of the first practices of my junior season, the coach had J.W. and me run 72 trap plays in a row. He still claims that was done so that we'd stop overplaying the trap. I don't buy it. It wasn't one of those situations where we stopped working on it once we got it right. We were doing it right a lot. I think he wanted to test our mettle.

After practice, players and other coaches were concerned because I looked weak and ill. Coach Pittman grabbed a barrel of ice water, snuck up behind me as I showered, and dumped it on my head. I shot up like a scared cat. It woke me up in a hurry, but I was so dehydrated I had to go to the hospital for treatment.

The next day, I returned to practice and told Coach Pittman, "I don't know what you are trying to accomplish, but I've been in way worse situations than the one I was in yesterday. Before I leave here, I'll be one of the best high school football players you ever coached."

He looked at me and with a sneer and said, "Son, you haven't even made the team yet."

That's one thing about Coach Pittman: even if you were a star, he treated you like everyone else. He kept us humble — or, as humble as possible. As he attests today, there was no way to humble me. I did not lack for confidence. I knew I was good.

"Well, that's not what I said," I replied. "I said before I leave your high school, I'll be one of the best high school players you ever coached."

Looking back, I'd say we were both right that week. I did become one of the best players he ever had. And damn it, no one in the state played the trap play better than I did. That season, I made first team all-county and all-state and was second team All-American as a defensive tackle.

It was crazy. Just a few years earlier, there was less than a handful of people in the world who cared about me or saw any potential in me. Then, suddenly, I was a football golden boy and everyone wanted to be my friend.

I'd be lying if I said I didn't love it. I enjoyed every minute of the attention I received. I never saw a reporter I didn't want to talk to. It's not just the on-field and on-court entertainment that draws me to sports. The games are great, but I also love everything that happens before and after the game. I loved watching that pre-game footage of Michael Jordan pulling up to the arena. I've always been fascinated by post-game press conferences. We know exactly what the reporters are going to ask and what the players are going to say, yet there remains an authentic drama as we watch the body language of the interviewee and try to read between the lines.

My favorite football coaches have larger-than-life personalities too — guys like Rex Ryan and Mike Ditka. I love the pageantry of sports as much as the competition, so when I had the opportunity to be part of the show, even as a high schooler, I relished it. It felt good to be special. It felt good to be in demand.

That demand grew during my junior season when Coach Pittman took me to a scouting combine in Jacksonville to further show off what I could do in front of recruiters.

I ran the 40-yard dash in 4.5 seconds, but when I told coach about my time, he didn't believe me. "You're lying," he repeated three times. "A kid who is six-foot-two, 275 pounds is not running a 4.5."

I kept telling him I did, so he asked the time-keeper for confirmation. Coach then said to me, "Son, you keep your grades up and your head on straight and keep working hard, and you are on your way. I promise that."

I took that to heart. I remembered the story of Michael Jordan as a high schooler writing down his goals and looking at them regularly for inspiration. On a regular basis, he would say things to himself like, "I'm going make the team next year," and "I'm going to be one of the best players."

On my cottage wall, I hung a dry-erase board on which I wrote motivational phrases like "Be a better person," "Grow into a better relationship with God," and "Be the best athlete possible."

My "unofficial" recruiting trips started that junior season. Unofficial means a recruit can visit the campus and discuss playing for the team, but he must foot the bill himself. The college could not kick in one penny for travel, lodging, or meal expenses. Mr. Blalock took care of expenses and traveled with me to the campuses.

My first unofficial trip was to Florida State University. Being that I was a lifelong fan of their athletic teams and because that was where top Suwannee players usually ended up, most people, including myself, figured that would ultimately be my pick.

What an experience. They played rivals University of Miami that weekend. They brought me into the locker room and then down onto the field before kickoff to look out into that stadium and feel the energy of nearly 80,000 rabid fans. Then they provided me with field-level seats, where I watched them retire the great Deion Sanders's jersey.

My next unofficial trip was to the University of South Carolina to meet with Coach Brad Holtz. When I got back to Live Oak, I told Coach Pittman that FSU and South Carolina seemed like great options.

"You're going get plenty of offers," he told me. "Take all your visits, even if some visits come after you know in your heart of hearts where you are going to end up. Have fun, son, and enjoy this time in your life because you may never have an experience like this again. Once you pick a college, you're not going to feel this special ever again, unless you become some big NFL free agent."

He's right. I don't know how recruiting trips feel to guys who grew up in affluent homes but for inner-city kids who have never been out of their state, this is their first chance to see different parts of the country. For kids who grew up believing they were nothing and who were treated like nothings by the power structure of their community, imagine suddenly having rich and powerful men from top universities call you every day, send you letters, kiss your butt, and tell you how special you are and how much they need you — man, it is something.

The best way I can explain it to someone who has never had a Division I school try to recruit them to play for one of their top athletic teams is to compare it to shopping for suits. You'll get good service if you go to a store and buy a suit off the rack. But that doesn't compare to having a suit custom tailored. Someone will fly in to sit down with you to go over fabrics, pick out linings, and measure you, and if one inch of that suit is not up to your standards, they'll fix it.

Now imagine someone getting that treatment who has never even bought a suit off the rack before. Imagine someone getting that treatment who spent much of his life being clothed out of Goodwill bins and hand-me-downs.

I took six official recruiting trips during my senior year — Florida State, University of Florida (of course), Tennessee, Notre Dame, Ohio State, and Georgia Tech.

Tennessee was the first. I had two hosts that weekend: Peyton Manning and Leonard Little.

The coaching staff's job is to sell you on the football. They walk you through their stadium and detail the history of the team, naming all its high points, and ask you to envision yourself playing in front of the tens of thousands of die-hard fans who live and breathe the team's colors. Those sell jobs always include a team uniform with your name on it. Even though you know what they are doing, it's hard to not get caught up in the moment.

The host's job is to sell you on that college's overall experience. They take you to the hot restaurants and the big parties. They introduce you to girls as the next great player. I swear I was ready to commit to Tennessee that weekend because it was my first time flying, because it was my first time outside of Florida, and, if I'm being honest, because of the girls. One of the Volunteers Girls I'd met was one of the most beautiful women I had ever seen, and she was talking to me! I was in love.

The recruiters knew what they were doing. There is no way such a beautiful woman would be talking to a high school kid. But then my flight home was delayed by a full day due to a snow storm. That killed the deal. I was a Florida boy. Snow? Hell no.

The same thing happened at Ohio State, where offensive lineman Orlando Pace was my host. I flew in the day before the Heisman Trophy was presented that year. The next day, Ohio State's Eddie George was the winner.

I bumped into Eddie in the gym on the day I was set to leave. Think about that — the dude was just named the best player in college and was back at the gym already. He refused to rest on his laurels.

Honestly, I was star struck. That was my first time ever meeting a Heisman winner. Plus, he was a beast — a total monster in the weight room.

The entire trip, Orlando Pace kept saying to me, "Hey, young fella, this cold weather isn't gonna get to you, is it?" After meeting Eddie George, my answer was creeping toward no.

But it again snowed on the day I was supposed to fly out. The delay was only hours long, but that was enough. The cold weather got to me. Sorry, Orlando.

My third visit was to Notre Dame. I did not have any plans to go there. Nothing against the school, but it's in the middle of nowhere, and by that time I had realized I wanted nothing to do with cold weather.

Still, it's Notre Dame. You can't blow off Notre Dame. If you're invited to that iconic campus, you make the trip.

I don't remember who my host was, but I'll never forget getting to chat with their legendary coach, Lou Holtz. And I'll never forget all the people who suddenly wanted to be my friend.

Once you are labeled a can't-miss prospect and possible NFL player, everyone — kids and adults alike — wants to get close to you. A professional athlete is considered an asset in one's inner circle, so people jockey to add you to theirs.

My advice to those going through the recruiting process: if someone was not part of your inner circle before you were thought of as a future professional athlete, don't let them in after.

Lebron James is a perfect example of how to handle success. He jumped right from high school to the NBA and became an overnight millionaire and household name. He probably had more leeches seeking to latch onto him than any other rookie professional athlete ever. Yet he has navigated stardom without a single personal scandal and has become a business mogul while still a player. He has done so by carefully picking the people who surround him. His inner circle is primarily made up of his childhood best friends because they loved him before he was rich and will always love him. He knows he can trust them.

You need to be careful as fame approaches because a lot of people who do not have your best interests in mind will enter into your life. Instead, they will only pretend to care about you while actually looking out for their own best interests.

My grandfather was one such man to me. Yeah, my mom's biological father.

He was never part of her life. He left my grandmother before my mom was born. Then one of my mom's friends mentioned she knew him and where he resided and that he wanted to talk. Intrigued, my mom agreed to meet her father.

She first introduced him to my brothers. Then she took him to watch one of my football games during senior year.

After the game, he waited for me outside the locker room and introduced himself. It was awkward. Not only had I never met him, but I had never really thought of him. Since I didn't have a father, not having a grandfather was never a big deal to me. He'd abandoned my mom, so I didn't trust him. That feeling got stronger during our initial conversation when he talked about being a big FSU fan and how he hoped to see me play there some day.

If my mom — who was the one who had been abandoned by him — was cool with him being part of my life, I figured I owed him the opportunity. And if he was willing to make things right with my mom, I'd give him a chance. Plus, he was nice to have around. He had money, and I had little.

He owned land that had a large population of trees that he sold to lumber yards. He also had plenty of rental properties that turned a profit. He'd come into town as often as he could and take me to the movies or out to dinner.

He would sometimes take me back to his hometown for the weekend.

He liked to impress me by taking me to collect rent at places that leased his properties. He paraded me around town by boasting to his friends, "This is my grandson. He's an All-American football player who everyone wants. You should see the recruiters coming at him."

He never mentioned once to his friends that we'd

only just met because he'd abandoned my mother when she was a kid.

He would push FSU on me throughout every visit. I don't think FSU administrators put him up to it, but I do think boosters or even just everyday fans he knew suggested he steer me toward the university they cheered for. I think he saw it as a feather in his cap and a way to feel big-time.

He was there with me during my official trip to FSU. He drove me, stayed with me all weekend, and hung out in the background when the coaching staff talked to me. He was trying to be *that* dude, pretending that he'd been there for me all along and had helped groom me into the athlete and young man that I was.

The thing is, no one can fool a kid who comes from a background like mine. The term "street smart" doesn't just mean we can survive in the ghetto. It also means we can sniff out a con a mile away. I knew my grandfather was up to something. I didn't call him out on it, but I pressed him in other ways. For instance, I let him know he was wrong to abandon my mother and asked him to explain why he did it.

"You know, it was just a certain situation came up," he stammered.

"Oh, yeah, what kind of situation?"

"Well, I can't go into detail about that," he said.

But I tried to be cool with him as long as he was willing to make good by my mom.

When it became apparent that he wasn't willing to do anything for her, I stopped giving him much time. He still came around from time to time for dinner, and we'd meet up sometimes on the weekend, but I would not let him become a fixture in my life. He was family by blood, but he was not my real family.

As I weathered the dark side of the recruiting storm, I watched as others failed to do so. I won't name names, so excuse the vagueness in my example.

There was a quarterback who played in my conference who could do it all. He could kick, punt, quarterback, receive, and play running back or any position on the defensive side. He was a Michael Vick–level athlete before we thought God had ever created such a specimen.

Every college in the nation wanted him when he was a junior. But he lost his way during his senior season. He felt he was untouchable. He thought he was so good that he didn't have to work hard anymore, that he could still succeed regardless. That was his demise.

Recruiters could sense that he had a weak work ethic and felt entitled. Couple those bad traits with his poor grades, and it was evident that his character was lacking. Top colleges bypassed him for players with lesser talent.

Instead of a major Division I school, he ended up at junior college. His attitude never improved, but his athleticism was so dominant there that a major university later gave him a chance. But due to his lack of work ethic, he never lived up to his potential. It was a real shame.

Luckily, I had the type of support staff I needed. During my senior year, I even added a few people to it.

The average stay at the Boys Ranch is 18 months. I was there for five years. I was doing so well that neither the ranch administrators nor my mother thought it was a good idea for me to return to South Florida.

During my senior year, I was allowed to move off campus, but I still had access to all the social services and facilities.

I lived with foster parents Romeo and Felicia Jean and their two small kids in Live Oak, and in exchange, they received some government funding to pay for my expenses. It was quite the experience. Mr. Jean was white. Mrs. Jean was Black. They lived in a brand-new double wide trailer. The kids shared one bedroom, and I got the other. They were a good family, and living that stereotypical family life kept me grounded.

Ms. Roy stayed on me too. Even though I was yet again not one of her students during my senior year, she would continually ask about my grades and remind me that I was one broken leg away from having only my mind to get me through life.

"What are you going to do if that happens?" she'd ask. "If you don't have your academics together, what are you going to realistically do? Football needs to be your plan B. School should always be your plan A."

Still, it was mostly Coach Pittman and Mr. Blalock who kept me in line. Coach Pittman and I were known to butt heads. He was hard on players, and I had an innate belief that I needed to protect the underdogs. I could take it when he was hard on me, but when he was hard on someone I felt could not handle it, I would go to that player's defense.

"You gotta learn when to stay outta things!" Coach would yell at me. "Stop stirring stuff up that doesn't concern you."

During my senior season, we were ranked seventh in the nation and had a big game coming up against Sarasota Riverview, the team that was ranked number one by *USA Today*. Coach and I got into it good at practice in the week leading up to the game. I thought we needed to do things one way. He wanted them done another. When I wouldn't let things be, he exploded. "You are done," he screamed. "You are not playing this week. Go sit your butt on the bench. If you wanna go to the game, you're gonna have to buy your own ticket and sit in the stands! And you can sit with the Sarasota fans because I don't even want you cheering for us!"

After practice, the defensive coordinator, Wade Beal, told Coach Pittman that they needed me. Well, Coach wouldn't budge. "I'm tired of him running his mouth. I've talked to him about this more than once," Coach Pittman said.

Coach Wade stayed on Coach Pittman until he relented. "If you want him to play, that is on you, and you let him know that. If he screws up, it's your fault. I will fire your butt, and you let Thaddeus know that."

As Coach Pittman would have said, "I was happier than a pig in slop," when I learned I could suit up. Then I was beat on the first two snaps I played. On the first, they ran a veer right at me, and I whiffed. On the next, the quarterback faked a hand off, pulled the ball back, and ran right at me. I missed again.

Coach Pittman called time out and sent Coach Wade onto the field. He didn't talk to a single player but me.

"Listen, mother f-er," he screamed into my face. "I fought for you. If you don't start playing, you're gonna get cut, and I'm gonna get fired. You need to step up. You're way too good to not step up, and we need you in the game."

On the third play, the quarterback tried to run by me again. It didn't go well for him. I hit him so hard that Coach Pittman thought I'd ended that poor guy's high school career.

We won the game in a blowout: 24–3.

Then there was the racial incident. "Boy" is what one wide receiver on my team kept calling me. He didn't mean "boy" in the same way I have written it throughout this book. Boy was not to denote I was a male kid. "Boy" was racially motivated.

My mom always told me, "Don't ever let anybody call you *boy*. You're a young man."

Remember history. "Boy" is what slave masters called the slaves in the field, even when those slaves were grown men. It was meant to demean them, to say they were not on the same mental level as the white adults. "Shut up, boy . . . Sit down, boy . . . Do your dance, boy."

I ignored the wide receiver for weeks. Instead of lashing out with my fists, I decided to just keep destroying him on the field during practice. His rage at getting beaten by a "boy" finally got to him. After beating him once again during Oklahoma drills, I laughed and said under my breath, "Who you calling 'boy'?"

"I'm talking to you, *N-word*," he growled, but he didn't say "N-word." He said the entire word.

There is no world in which I am going to let any person talk to me that way, then or now. I charged, taking him down hard, and he quickly realized he'd messed with the wrong guy.

The other players on the team broke up the fight, and Coach Pittman gave a fiery but — what I considered — paint by numbers, blasé, "That's not how we talk on this team" speech.

I lost my temper even more because I thought that

Coach Pittman needed to be more forceful. "You're a racist," I yelled to the coach.

I don't think I'd ever seen Coach so mad. He grabbed me by the shoulder pad and yanked me to the sideline where he could talk to me one-on-one.

"Son, you better never say I am racist again," he screamed up at me. I stood a good four or five inches taller than him. "There are a lot of nasty things that can be said about me that are true, but that ain't one of them. You ever say that again, and we got a problem."

He was right. He was far from a racist. I had lost my cool and said something I didn't mean, and I felt bad about it.

We continued to butt heads after that, but only about football. Today he remains a friend.

After hearing of that incident, Mr. Blalock reminded me that because I was Black, there would always be certain people who'd have preconceived notions of who I was. No matter how much I excelled in football or school, to some, I'd be nothing more than the N-word. I could be smarter and more athletic than someone, but he or she would still think they were better than me because they are white. Because of that, I could not make the same mistakes the white kids made. I was held to a higher standard, and he continually pushed me to expect more of myself.

It is a sad reality that people do not want to address or discuss, but it is the truth. On many occasions, if a Black kid raised by abusive and addict parents who are in and out of jail commits a crime, there are some people who will label him or her a "thug" and seek out proof to back that point of view. When a white kid from that same situation commits a crime, those same people will describe that kid as being "lost in the system," and seek out what went wrong in rearing that child.

Mr. Blalock would also not allow me to paint a wide brush over the country and look at all white people as racist. The way I responded to Coach Pittman was wrong. If I want respect, I need to give respect, he said. I needed to stop thinking that everyone in Live Oak was a redneck. If they were, would Mr. Blalock had been elected superintendent? I needed to be more open-minded and accepting of everyone, he explained, because I'd eventually work with people from all walks of life. Whether it be on a sports team or in an organization, I'd be working with people that are different than me, different in thought, different in religion, different in political stance, different in race, different in sexual orientation.

And at the end of the day, I have to remember that I am neither lesser than no one nor better than anyone. I needed to be proud to be an African American but remember that I am part of a bigger and more important race — the human race. We are all the same. Mr. Blalock was the first adult to talk to me about race as though I was an adult.

It's a lesson I missed out on as a young child who, for whatever reason, specifically needed a father figure to teach me that lesson. My anger may have lessened if I'd received it earlier.

I lived up to the hype that senior year. I was first team all-state. *Parade* and *USA Today* both named me an All-American. I was named to the Bluechip Illustrated Dream Team. SuperPrep ranked me the second-best defensive lineman in the country. The National Recruiting Advisor ranked me the second top defensive tackle prospect. In both instances, Marcus Stroud was ranked ahead of me.

By the end of that season, I'd narrowed my choice down to Florida State and University of Florida. Everyone thought it would be FSU, and I did love my interactions with the university.

Coach Bobby Bowden was an awesome man. He was very grandfatherly in his approach. There were rumors even back then that his years of coaching were behind him, he was nothing more than a figurehead, and he'd soon be retiring, so signing with FSU was a risk. I never bought into any of that nor did it impact my decision.

Andre Wadsworth, who ended up being selected third overall in the 1998 NFL Draft, was my host, and he was someone I idolized. He was a walk-on at FSU who then earned an athletic scholarship. Of all the stars at FSU I could have partnered with, he was the most appropriate because I had made it known that academics were just as important as football to me, and he had the same belief. I didn't want to be one of those dudes who earned a degree in a subject just because it was the easiest route to take, only to have no use for that degree if the NFL did not work out.

Ultimately, while FSU gave me a good and earnest showing in that respect, University of Florida topped them. My host for my junior year visit was Kevin Carter, whom I'd watch play at nearby Lincoln High School, and whom I considered a good friend and role model.

He was later drafted number six overall by the Rams in 1995, and he knew during my visit he'd go at least that high, possibly higher. Still, he majored in pharmacy and didn't put down the books or switch to an easier major because a contract worth millions of dollars was in his future. That impressed me more than his first team All-American status.

I fell in love with Coach Steve Spurrier at the University of Florida from the start. He reminded me very much of Mr. Monogue — he was that guy you wanted to hang out with, and you knew he loved hanging out with his players.

He was also very much like me — honest and forthcoming. He said that he was not going to guarantee me playing time, but if I looked at the depth chart, I had a good chance of earning some time as a freshman. He said, "Look, I'm not one of those guys who is going to kiss your ass. You know what Florida has to offer. We would love for you to come and be a part of it. If you choose to come here — great. If you choose to go somewhere else — we will have fun beating your ass."

What sealed it for me was Coach Spurrier's trips to meet with me in Live Oak. Other coaches came to see me too, but Coach Spurrier's visits were more special. Typically, the only recruits he left campus to meet were the quarterbacks and offensive players. His assistants were charged with other recruiting trips to high school towns. He made the exception for me. That meant a lot.

On January 30, 1996, at a press conference in Live Oak, I signed my letter of intent to go to the University of Florida. That was a big day, and little of that has to do with football. It meant I'd be the first person in my immediate family to go to college. I felt as if I were breaking a generational curse for my brothers and, later, our children.

I graduated high school with high honors. I wasn't valedictorian or class president, but I was asked to give a speech at graduation anyway. I read a poem I wrote. I can't remember exactly how it went, but it detailed all the good times we had in the school hallways, our accomplishments in the classrooms and on the field, and I finished it up with my imitation of Fire Marshall Bill from *In Living Color* — "Alrighty then" and that goofy laugh.

I did it. I graduated. I was going to college to forge a path and become my own man.

My own man — I stress that phrase. Let me rewind back to recruiting season. The day before I was set to announce I'd attend the University of Florida, another head coach flew into Live Oak to make one last pitch.

"Where did I go wrong?" he asked. "How can I correct it? Tell me, what did they give you at Florida that I didn't give you. What is Coach Spurrier paying you?"

He was insinuating that Florida had bought me. That was the furthest thing from the truth.

To those recruits who are considering taking such offers or to parents of recruits who are pushing their kids to take such offers — DON'T DO IT. As a former Division I athlete, I am aware that such athletes collectively bring in billions of dollars to universities. So, I agree that Division I athletes should receive financial compensation. But, right now, it is illegal, and I do not want men and women to jeopardize their careers.

The moment players accept one penny, they not only put their career as a student and an athlete in jeopardy but also put their university at risk to receive sanctions, suspensions, and public humiliation. A player who takes that money is selfish, because that decision could negatively impact their teammates and friends.

I understand that it's hard. Someone offers you new shoes or a new car on the same day that you stood in the free lunch line, and you live with your single mom in a tiny roach-infested apartment, you're going to be tempted. But don't be; do not take a penny. If you get caught, you will lose your scholarship. If you lose your scholarship, your college career may be over. No matter how sure of a thing you may think you are, there are no guarantees in life. You can't be certain you'll get drafted in the first, second, or third round, and there is no guarantee you will go pro at all. Even if you do, you don't know how long you'll be there. And even if you have a full career, you're still retired at a young age. What are you going to do with the rest of your life? Unless you have that education, you will not have a fulfilling post-athletic career.

It is up to the adults who mentor star athletes to remind them of that fact. I am lucky that I had coaches and mentors who believed in tough love. I detest those who pamper star child athletes. When you do, you prevent them from learning to deal with the realities of the world. There is going to be a point in that person's life when ability is not going to be the key determining factor in whether they succeed. Instead, their attitude and character will dictate success. And when you don't teach a kid how to be humble and how to be respectful to their teammates, coaches, fans, and the game, the child will lack that needed character.

Sports don't owe you a thing, and the games will always move on without you, no matter how good you are. I was a hell of a player at Suwannee High School. I also haven't played there in decades. And the football team is still playing games and winning without me.

I'll be fine if I break my leg tomorrow and can no longer be a WWE Superstar. I'm college educated. I'm in a good financial position because of that education. I am set for life, not because of my muscles, but because of my brain.

CHAPTER 10

On January 14, 2015, at the Nationwide Arena in Columbus, Ohio, my WWE tag team partner, Darren Young, and I were crowned the WWE Tag Team Champions when we defeated The New Day at the *Money in the Bank* pay-per-view. That was the first WWE title that I'd ever held. And it felt amazing.

For those who don't understand the wrestling business, from an entertainment standpoint, yes, we are storytellers and the stories that we tell are predetermined. Yet the actions and athletic feats that are performed are very real, which is why there is a disclaimer on TV prior to every show, telling people not to try at home what we do every night. Although it may be predetermined, the opportunity to carry the title of champion in this business is a very real honor. When you're selected to carry a title in WWE, it means the company trusts you as someone who can represent WWE both on television as a character and in public as an ambassador.

When WWE gave us the news that the story we would be telling that night in Columbus would end with us being crowned champions, it was the proudest I'd been to that point in my WWE career.

While some of my peers have held multiple championships, that has not been the case for me. But to me, being a WWE Superstar is not just about championships, which is why I will reiterate something I wrote in chapter one. You know me as Titus O'Neil, but that is just a character I play on television. My real name is Thaddeus Bullard, and I have achieved plenty of things outside of the ring that I am proud of.

I have been honored by the Reverend Jessie Jackson as part of the PUSH Coalition as a Humanitarian of the Year Award winner, tabbed as the 2015 MEGA Dads Celebrity Dad of the Year, received a Drum Major for Justice Award from the Martin Luther King Parade Foundation, and am the only person to be named both an honorary Hillsborough County Deputy and an honorary member of the Tampa Police Department. I could list other honors, but I think being tabbed as one of *Ebony* magazine's Power 100 List in 2018 sums up a lot in regards to my contributions to the greater good of others.

There is no question that I love being a WWE Superstar. I continue to strive to be the best WWE Superstar I can be. But I have also been very adamant, much like I was with football, that I am so much more.

There is one piece of advice I give to everyone who strives to live a successful, happy life of peace: never allow what you do for a living determine who you are for a living. Perform in your career to the highest of your ability and then use that success to help those around you.

How I live my life has always been more important to me than what I do for a living. Every WWE Superstar, including myself, loves to hold a championship, but there are only so many championship titles to go around. And, quite honestly, we have to keep in perspective that those championships are part of a television show — the longest running weekly episodic television series of all time, by the way. It's sports entertainment.

There have been times when some wrestlers put way too much stock on winning championships. In my opinion, some believe that winning makes them the most important person on the roster. But the reality is that all of us are important. We're all part of a diverse roster of sports entertainers; we're a team of characters who people from all walks of life can cheer or boo.

With that comes responsibility: you must have integrity and character. I'm not talking about WWE personas, but real-life character — meaning you're on time, respectful, understanding, responsible, genuine, and welcoming. You need to lead by example. If your example is strong and consistent enough, it is my belief you will be fortunate enough to be a role model to both children and adults.

When you leave this earth, there should be a sense of loss. But, honestly, if the only thing people remember you by is the title of your profession, then there is a good chance your life was not as fulfilling as it could have been. In my opinion, if we focus more on the real issues and improving the living conditions of those who are less fortunate, we all become champions in our own way.

It was while I was a student at the University of Florida that the idea that my off-field performance was just as important as on-field accolades had become so ingrained in me. They work hand in hand. Although fans focus only on tackles and touchdowns, the student athlete's experience at college should mean something more. The "student" in student athlete comes first for a reason. Only a fool would put all of their effort into athletics while not putting an equal effort into academics and focusing on growing personally and professionally.

From the moment I graduated high school, I knew that the University of Florida would set me on an exciting and prosperous new path. I couldn't wait to get to Gainesville.

But unlike leaving Boyton Beach, when I was in such a rush that I stopped to see only my grand-mother, leaving Live Oak was difficult. I made sure to visit, thank, and say goodbye to everyone who had a positive impact on me.

I would miss everyone, but I was also excited. I was going to the University of Florida! I was going to the Swamp; I was going to be a Gator; I was going to be playing football for one of the most successful college football coaches of all time. I wouldn't have to wait long to start my collegiate football career. Workouts started just weeks after my high school graduation. Nor did I want to wait long to start my collegiate academic career.

I was well aware of the challenges of being a student athlete, especially at a school like the University of Florida, which boasted elite academic and athletic programs. Balancing a full class schedule while playing for a national championship contender football team *is* difficult. I decided to wade into the stream rather than jump into the ocean.

I signed up for four summer classes: English 1101 and Math 1101 in the first summer semester and English 1102 and Math 1102 in the second semester. Doing so while participating in summer football training, I figured, would help me acclimate before I was hit with a full load of classes and the rigors of a season.

There were two choices for summer football training: a 6 a.m. workout or a 3 p.m. workout. I decided to go with the afternoon option so that I could take a morning class. I found out very quickly that the afternoon training session was much harder. The Florida heat was at its apex during the afternoon session. Anyone who has ever gone on an afternoon jog in Florida knows what I am talking about.

At the beginning, the training sessions mostly focused on conditioning and strength. We lifted four times a week. Wednesdays included a 12-minute run or some other form of intense cardio. The 12-minute run was supposed to be the most difficult challenge of all our workouts. In 12 minutes or under, linemen had to run six and a half laps; linebackers, seven and a half; and wide receivers, running backs, quarterbacks, and defensive backs, eight and a half. I chose to run with the defensive backs. I always did, even when we ran the 100-yard sprints. I loved the challenge.

There is always going to be competition when you put a group of elite athletes together. We'd see someone push a certain weight on the bench and want to top it. Someone would hit a certain mark in conditioning, and we'd want to top that. Practice would be over, and we'd hit the basketball court and compete in pickup games.

I enjoyed the summer classes too. The professors were cool — they treated us like men and women rather than kids. The football team made sure players had whatever outside assistance we needed — tutors, study hall, whatever it took. If an athlete fails out of a

Division I school, it is their own fault. They have the support system to succeed; they just need to have the desire to take advantage of it.

Of course, I saw players who didn't take schooling seriously. They were just happy to be on campus. They were going out and partying and hanging out late. I appreciated where I was, and I also knew I was there primarily to get an education. Football was how I was paying for my schooling — it did not take precedence over my studies. If I played well enough to get a shot at the NFL, great. Even then, I needed to be ready for life after professional football. I knew my body wouldn't hold up forever. I needed an exit plan.

Stories of failures of the past were enough to motivate me. I had heard of too many players boasting that they didn't need to study because they were going to the NFL after college and would be set for life. But then they either wouldn't make it or would have a short-lived professional career and blow their earnings quickly because they didn't have the education needed to manage that money.

I still went out and had fun, of course. I was in college after all. But I knew not to overdo it. I knew to prioritize school first, football second, and collegiate fun third. I'm not saying that summer was easy. It wasn't. My body was hurt and sore on most mornings. I'd be so mentally and physically exhausted that I'd want to toss my alarm clock out the window when it went off at 5 a.m. As the season approached, however, it all seemed worth it. We were ranked pre-season number 4 and predicted to win the NCAA Southeastern Conference.

The team was stacked: Danny Wuerffel, Ike Hilliard, Fred Taylor, Mike Green, Jacquez Green, Reggie McGrew, Jevon Kearse, Tim Beauchamp, Willie Cohen, Willie Rodgers, the list went on and on.

I was only a freshman, but I expected to get some playing time. The coaches never promised me, but they said I'd have the opportunity to earn it, and I knew I was playing well enough to do just that.

Then, just weeks before the season started, news came. My advisor called me into his office and told me I was academically ineligible to play football. That also meant I would not have a scholarship. My season was over, and my semester was possibly finished too.

"How am ineligible?" I asked. "I took four summer classes and received good grades in each."

It wasn't my college grades, he explained, but my high school marks. He then asked if anyone had ever altered any of my grades at Suwannee to benefit me.

"Absolutely not," I said.

He explained that the transcripts that were originally sent to the NCAA clearing house to prove my eligibility showed I had received a C in English at Suwannee. Yet, my final high school transcripts listed that grade as a B. Because of that discrepancy, the NCAA was questioning my transcripts in full. After the meeting, I went back to my dorm and took the frustration out on my wall by throwing a haymaker at it. The wall won that fight. The wall always wins. So did the NCAA. They refused to think rationally about the accusation levied against me.

It didn't matter that I'd scored very high on the ACTs. It didn't matter that I'd earned good grades in my summer courses. All that mattered to the NCAA was dealing with the illusion of cheating. The truth is that there was a discrepancy in my English grade. It had changed from a C to a B. But there was nothing unlawful about it. It was nothing more than a simple mistake. My high school guidance counselor sent the transcript in too early. When she did, I had a C in English. Then I took my final, aced it, and pulled the grade up to a B. That was the grade listed on my final transcript.

The NCAA would not budge, so I agreed to retake the ACT. I scored even higher than before and expected to rejoin the team. The NCAA still refused to reinstate me. Why? Because I'd taken the entrance exam after I'd already taken summer classes, so that score was meaningless.

I was not alone in my anger. Reading through old newspaper clips, almost everyone took my side and blasted the NCAA for their decision. It was obvious to anyone with a brain that this was wrong and that I deserved to be on the field.

I have no proof, but I think someone at my high

school wanted to sabotage my collegiate career. I don't mean that they purposely sent in my grades early, knowing that my final exam would pull my English score up and create the illusion of cheating. I think someone saw the discrepancy and, even though they knew I was innocent, they tipped off the NCAA anyway, hoping it would hurt me. Most of the faculty at my school were FSU fans and they expected me to go there. When I chose Florida, they were upset. Making it difficult for me to become a University of Florida Gator was their revenge.

That incident was an ugly reminder of how unfair the governing bodies of college sports could be. I had done nothing wrong, but I lost out on my freshman season of football because a clerical error had created a mirage of impropriety. I was unjustly made to appear like some jock trying to skate through the system.

The NCAA made me a deal, though. I could be reinstated for my sophomore season if I earned good grades. Then, if I could graduate college in three years, I could get my lost year of eligibility back and play another season after I earned my bachelor's degree. If that makes zero sense to you, join the club. All these years later, I still don't understand why they thought I needed to graduate in three years when so many students take five or even six years without the added responsibility and workload of being a Division I football player at a major university. That so-called nice gesture further infuriated me. The NCAA was trying to come off as the good guy by appearing to be taking the high road.

I had people telling me I should sue the NCAA. Get my money, they told me, and prove to everyone that the NCAA was wrong. And I was dead set on proving they were wrong to assume I was some deadbeat jock who was looking for the easy road in life. But I would not do so by suing them.

Instead, I wrote the NCAA a letter that said I didn't know what they were trying to accomplish, but I would graduate in three years and send them a copy of my degree. I told them, I'll go on to grad school or law school, and I'll be the example of what they should be celebrating and not hindering, as far as student athletes are concerned. Finally, I wrote, I would overcome whatever obstacles they threw at me.

I took out student loans and a Pell Grant to make tuition and was in class by the time the school year started. I lost my dorm room during the investigation since it seemed I would no longer be a student, so I found an off-campus apartment.

Mr. Blalock helped me to buy a car so that I could drive back to Live Oak whenever I felt the need to get off campus. On weekends when I was too busy to leave but needed a father, Mr. Blalock would stay at my apartment. On a few occasions, Mr. Blalock picked me up and took me to football games at Florida A&M University.

I was mad. It hurt. I missed my teammates. I missed playing football. To make matters worse, they won the national title that year. It was impossible to escape the coverage. Turn on the TV, they were talking about Gator football. Pick up a newspaper, there was Gator football on the front page. Walk around campus, everyone was talking Gator football.

I refused to let that hurt lead to my demise. Instead, like when Michael Jordan was cut from his varsity team, I used it as fuel. I finished my freshman year with good grades and was allowed back on the team for my sophomore season.

Coach Spurrier was so impressed with my work ethic and maturity during my freshman year that he rewarded me with his retired number 11 for my sophomore season.

"We're going to throw him number eleven," coach told reporters. "We think it will look pretty good coming around the corner — like slam, number eleven."

Slam was right. I got into a fight in my first practice back.

It was with an offensive lineman who was mad because I beat him first with a hump move and then on the next play with a bull rush, both of which were patented by the great Reggie White. The lineman grabbed my face mask when I bull rushed him again on the third play. The whistle blew the play dead and he then shoved me. We threw some blows, and Coach Spurrier rushed over to break it up with a stern lecture.

"Guys, we don't need this," he yelled. "You're teammates. And you could hurt yourselves. What happens if you break your hand on a helmet? Is that how you want your season to end? Is that how you want to remember this season?"

He was right, so cooler heads prevailed, and today I am proud of how my college career is recalled by alumni.

As a University of Florida football player, I am remembered as a Gator Great. But football alone never defined me. The man I was off the field defined me, and that year-long break from football and the drive to beat the NCAA and the way they stereotyped me helped to instill that lesson in me.

Just as I promised the NCAA, I earned my undergraduate degree in three years — criminology, with a minor in sociology. That allowed me to spend my fourth year working toward my masters in higher education. My major was inspired by my time working for the law firm of Schackow & Mercadante during my freshman year. It was through this experience that I got an inside look at how the legal system treats the less fortunate.

Law firm partner Stephen Mercadante was once the catcher for the Gators' baseball team. The other partner, Gerald Schackow, once played quarterback for the University of Hawaii. The two of them were very much into collegiate sports. Schackow, in particular, had grown close with the University of

Florida's athletic director Jeremy Foley, with whom he ran marathons.

Just prior to my freshman year, Foley had approached the law firm about starting an internship program for student athletes who had an interest in a career in the legal field. Andy Brandi, who was tennis coach at the University of Florida, had read about my plight in the local newspapers and reached out to me. He too was friends with Schackow and Mercadante and said they were willing to give me a job as a law clerk.

The law firm paid me $12 an hour. The work was easy — picking up files, dropping off files at the courthouse, taking notes during depositions, stuff like that. To this day, I remain close with the Schackow family. On a few occasions since I graduated, I had friends in the Gainesville area in need of assistance for minor real estate issues. The firm has always stepped up.

I do my best to return the favor. A few years ago, for example, he had clients who were a mother and son involved in a car accident. To break the tension with the nervous young boy, Mr. Schackow asked if he liked sports. No, his mother replied, all he watches is WWE. Mr. Schackow asked who his favorite Superstar was. Oddly enough, it was me. So he put me on the phone with the kid. Mr. Schackow still maintains that is the happiest he has ever seen an injured client.

Mr. Schackow had courtside season tickets to Gators basketball and, even after I graduated and became a WWE Superstar, if I was in town, he would take me with him. After the games, as kids would yell "Titus!" and line up for my autograph, he would jokingly tell them that he used to get away with yelling at me. The truth is, he never yelled at me once. Instead, everyone at the firm took me under their wings while I worked for them.

They knew I was thirsty for knowledge and was not some dumb jock getting a handout. They regularly schooled me on the ins and outs of the cases they were working on and taught me how the court system operated. Mr. Schackow took on mostly personal injury matters but also did some criminal cases. He called it "street law," meaning he wanted to help the area's most vulnerable residents. He had a soft spot for people who came from the streets or who were one missed paycheck away from living on the streets. These were the type of people who couldn't afford to pay a simple ticket or the court costs that come with fighting a larger infraction. If he thought that they were innocent, he would work within their means, no matter what that was.

That job further opened my eyes to the reality of the legal system. It proved to me that if you have money, you have a better chance of beating the legal system. If you don't have money, you're in trouble, unless you find an attorney like Mr. Schackow.

Watching Mr. Schackow further inspired me to help others and to fight for those who have no one else to fight on their behalf.

I got active in the community. I volunteered at St. Francis House, which feeds and clothes the homeless. Everyone should spend time doing such volunteer work — the sooner you do, the sooner you'll learn that most negative views of the homeless are wrong. Not everyone who is homeless is lazy. Not everyone who is homeless is a drug addict or an alcoholic. Most have been boxed in by a bad break and are struggling to find the door out.

Then, when my freshman year was up, the NCAA told me I could no longer work at the law firm. Collegiate athletes on scholarship could not have jobs — just yet another stupid NCAA rule that began with the right intentions but the way it was enforced punished the wrong people.

Before banning student athletes from working, some were abusing the system, especially those at major Division I programs. A normal student working at a car wash might get minimum wage. If a booster owns the business, an NCAA football star who is on television every Saturday might get $100 an hour and never have to wash a car. Instead of governing the boosters, the NCAA decided to punish the athletes.

Not every NCAA athlete comes from a well-to-do two-parent family who can financially support them. There are many who come from backgrounds like mine — raised by a single parent on welfare and food stamps. The NCAA was telling student athletes like me that if we wanted to take our boyfriend or girlfriend to the movies, too bad — not unless our parents sent us money.

I understand student athletes on scholarships are getting a free college education. But the NCAA has made billions off of their talents. The give and take is not proportional. Players should get paid, period. But back then, the NCAA was adamant: players could not get paid for their on-field work, and they couldn't get paid if they wanted to work off the field either.

When I returned to campus for my sophomore year, I sought to right that wrong. I became part of the University Athletic Association Board that petitioned our school administration. That organization joined students at other SEC schools who were doing the same. Together, we earned a small victory. The NCAA gave in and said student athletes could earn a maximum of $2,000 a semester and $4,000 a year.

My junior year, in the spring of 1999, I pledged the Omega Psi Phi fraternity, one of the largest and most prestigious African American fraternities in the nation. Being part of it remains one of my great honors. Brothers include civil rights icon Jessie Jackson, former president of the NAACP Roy Wilkins, NBA legends Michael Jordan and Shaquille

O'Neal, comedian Steve Harvey — a real who's who of respected individuals. Omega Psi Phi had been suspended on my campus a few years earlier for hazing infractions. My four-person pledge class was its first since the ban, so we made up the entire representation of that fraternity at our school. But the four of us turned our fraternity into a powerful on-campus force in 2000.

Yohance was president of Savant UF, a leadership honor society I was also a member of. Archie was vice president of the campus's Black Student Union. Dajuan was vice president of the campus NAACP, and I was vice president of the student body government. My time as vice president was my best experience on campus.

Politics at the University of Florida had an ugly history of backroom deals being made to put a thumb on the student government. At the center of it was an organization known as Florida Blue Key. Founded in 1923, it is one of the state's most prestigious leadership honor societies. Past members include the likes of former governors Lawton Chiles and Bob Graham.

Come election time, Florida Blue Key leaders would bring certain members together in unofficial meetings to pick a slate of candidates. They'd choose from a cross section of campus leaders who collectively could bring in votes from a variety of demographics. Blue Key could then set the student agenda for the year.

This system came tumbling down in 1998 when the courts found the organization liable in the defamation of Charles Grapski. In 1995, as he ran for student body president against the Blue Key slate, posters were circulated around campus that falsely accused him of being a child molester. He blamed Blue Key, the courts agreed, and the way they controlled the elections was made public. By 2000, Blue Key no longer wielded as much power, which allowed a ticket like the one I was part of to form and win.

I was a member of Florida Blue Key, but was not part of that former system. The same could be said about George Kramer. He was elected treasurer in 1999 and sought to ascend to presidency the following year. To do so, he needed to put together a slate of candidates who, like Blue Key used to do, could pull in voters from all demographics.

Kramer and I shared a common friend — Jocelyn Moore, who was vice president in 1999. She came to me in 2000 and asked if I would be interested in running as vice president on George's ticket. She thought I could help Kramer win the presidency due to my ties to the Black fraternities and being a football player. The Black fraternities and the more traditional mostly white fraternities did not typically mix. And University of Florida football stars had a history of success in student politics. My fellow Tampa resident Brad Culpepper, for instance, was vice president from 1991 to 1992.

Plus, my associations aside, I had a larger-than-life presence on campus. My WWE personality is just an extension of who I really am. I was big man — both literally and figuratively — on campus.

I had zero interest in politics, I informed my friend Jocelyn. Politicians were fake cardboard cut-outs who couldn't be trusted. I wanted nothing to do with that.

That is why they wanted me, she said. I was known for being a real straight shooter. If your breath stunk, I'd tell you.

They needed someone like me to be an outspoken and trusted face for what they wanted to accomplish. They knew that students would believe me when I told them that something would get done. I would not have to back any platform that I was not comfortable backing, and I could help choose areas the student government decided to help. With that, I was on board.

University of Florida elections are serious business. Elected officials controlled a $9.5 million budget to fund student activities. I'd estimate our main opponents spent over $100,000 during the election. They not only ran ads on the campus radio and television stations and in the newspaper, they also broadcast commercials on cable.

We spent too. Not as much, but close, and all of it was raised through donations from students and their parents, alumni, and local businesses, all of whom supported our vision for the campus. And unlike our opponents, we stuck to campus media outlets.

We campaigned the old-fashioned way: we hit the streets. We started by talking to the campus groups — fraternities, sororities, religious student groups, minority student groups, everyone. It was all about grass roots coalition building. We went to every major event on campus. We stood in the middle of campus and shook hands. If there had been a baby nearby, I'd have kissed it.

Our diversity was our strength. George was Caucasian, I was African American, and our candidate for treasurer, Anna Maria Garcia, was Hispanic, but we were each popular among all student demographics. Our message was populist in tone. In the past, the student activity budget was mostly portioned out to the student groups, but not every student was part of a campus organization. That $9.5 million came from student tuition — didn't everyone deserve to enjoy the spoils, we asked.

Our promises included extending the hours of the "Later Gator" bus that took students around Gainesville. As it was, the bus could drop them off at bars, but it didn't run late enough to take them home. And we promised to throw free campus concerts boasting major diverse musical talents.

We offered traditional platform bullet points too. I wanted to better fund the minority student unions, for instance, and we told the student body that just as our ticket brought a prominent white student, a prominent Black student, and a prominent Hispanic student together, we would do our best to bridge what we perceived as a growing divide between the minority and white students.

I have to be honest, though — while I was in the race because I wanted to bring positive change to the campus, once that election began, it was the competition that drove me.

It was a different feeling than what I experienced on the football field, but it drove me just the same. Along with following the standings in the newspaper to see how other teams were doing, I read about our opponents' campaign stops and promises. Just as I would check box scores, I was checking polling statistics. Just as I would watch game tapes and go to practices, I was preparing for debates.

I loved the debates, and I was good at them. My straightforward and colorful personality shined on that stage when I told the student body that we needed to do more to make their college experience enjoyable. I was assertive when I said we needed better lighting on campus to combat a rash of assaults on women.

In the end, politics is more about attitude than substance. Look at national politicians — they all basically say the same thing. It's a popularity contest.

Voters flock to the candidates who look better, talk better, and present themselves better overall. I was confident in our platform, and I was confident that my ability to put myself over far exceeded that of my opponents.

The election went into a runoff that included us. Then, with nearly 40,000 votes cast, we won by a razor-thin margin of around 200 — a true state of Florida election result.

There was one particular opponent I hated. I took such joy in seeing him concede the election to us and make one of those BS "I really hope we can work together to better the campus" statements. I graciously accepted, but I wanted to dance in his face.

To kick off the following school year, we had to speak at a pep rally welcoming all the new students. Over 10,000 young men and women packed into the Stephen C. O'Connell Center. I'd played football in front of tens of thousands of screaming fans who lived and died with my every movement on the field, but this was way different. It was my first time front and center with such a crowd, and I loved it.

When the semester got rolling, so did we. Remember those campaign promises we made? We lived up to all of them. We extended the Later Gator bus until the bars let out. We brought in diverse talent for campus concerts. In the past, the University of Florida student government only booked bands like the Smashing Pumpkins. They are a great band, but we added more diversity and unified the student body by booking acts like OutKast, Ludacris, Nelly, and Snoop Dogg.

OutKast performed at a party held at George's Theta Chi fraternity house. Black and white students alike flocked to the show. George remembers it as the first truly diverse party held at his fraternity house while he was a member.

Snoop performed at the Black Student Union's Step Show Weekend at the Stephen C. O'Connell Center. This was not an event typically attended by white students, but they were there that year to see Snoop.

Hotel rooms were slim that weekend, though. So, while most of Snoop's entourage and the other performers stayed at a hotel, Snoop stayed at my off-campus house. It didn't hurt that, thanks to my roommate, our pad was pretty sweet.

Snoop and I hit it off, and he then decided to stay an extra day and hang at my fraternity's barbeque. We've been friends ever since.

It's funny how life goes. Today, Snoop's cousin Mercedes Varnado — otherwise known as WWE Superstar Sasha Banks — is not only my co-worker but someone I'm so close with, I consider her to be my little sister.

While that was a cool highlight of my time as vice president, my top accomplishments are those times I took on the administration and forced them to right a wrong. For instance, there were serious discussions going on about closing the Black and Hispanic Student Unions and merging them into one that represented all minorities, due to budget cuts. That was not going to happen on my watch. The University of Florida was already a predominantly white university — shutting down the student unions of minorities wasn't going to help us feel more welcome, that's for sure.

Thanks in large part to our student government, the unions stayed open and money was budgeted to renovate their buildings.

Then there was the time we helped the janitors. Certain professors were complaining about the janitorial schedule. They didn't want someone coming into their classroom during the day to mop the floors and empty the trash. The janitors didn't do that while class was in session. But the professors would be in the room, grading papers or preparing lesson plans, and felt uncomfortable with a janitor in there too.

In response, the university shifted many janitorial schedules from day to night. To add insult to injury, the school also cut their salaries by 10 percent. I'd grown close to a few of the janitors; we'd joke around and talk football, and I treated them the same way I'd want someone to treat my mother. After the scheduling and salary decision was made, I overheard the janitors speaking with anger and disgust — and rightfully so. I promised them I'd do something to help.

I met with a few of my teammates, other high-profile students, and my student government and told them that we were in a position to help the janitors and that it was our duty to do so.

We started speaking on their behalf throughout campus and lobbied the administration. It all culminated on the day I personally spoke in front of the school administration.

"You want men and women who are forty-five, fifty, fifty-five, or sixty years old — many of whom are minorities — to take trash out at night on a dimly lit college campus?" I asked. "We have students who are being attacked on campus, and now you want to throw older people in harm's way too? If college kids are struggling to protect themselves, how do you think a grandmother will do?"

I then asked one administrator, "How old is your mom?"

He replied, "Sixty-three."

"We have some people who work here who are sixty-three," I said. "How would you feel if your mom was a janitor here and was working afternoons and then had her schedule shifted, but she had no say in the matter? What about those janitors who are single parents with kids who depend upon them being home at night? What if that parent cannot afford a babysitter or doesn't have family to look after that child at night?"

The administrators in the meeting put on their best "caring voices" and said, "We see where you're going."

"No," I shot back, "I'm not asking you to see where I am going. I want to know how you think it would affect your single parent mother?"

"It would impact her badly," one administrator said. "For some people, it would be very detrimental to their household."

"OK," I said. "Now imagine that for the four hundred to five hundred people you just made this decision for. I am not here demanding that you do this or that. What I am asking is that you put yourself in their shoes and contemplate if you are doing the right thing. We're all human beings, and if you are affected by my words, then imagine the realities that these men and women face. I can't tell the administration what to do. I *will* tell the entire student body that I not only think your decision should be flipped but also that the janitors deserve a raise."

The janitors had their old schedules restored, and they were given back the 10 percent of their salary that had been taken away.

I made a difference and it felt good. It felt better than winning the tag team title.

My college experience at the University of Florida allowed me to grow in many ways, both on and off the field. I gained a better understanding of using my platform as an athlete to encourage and foster growth and awareness to various causes. I also gained a better understanding of my purpose and my ability to draw people from all walks of life together by helping others to focus on the issues that unite us and not the differences that separate us.

In August 2000, I graduated from the University of Florida.

When I received my diploma, just about everyone who had helped me get to that point came out to cheer me on. My mom was there, of course. The Blalock family was there, as were Mr. Schackow and Mr. Bouchard and a host of others from the ranch.

I was happy to have such support, but I also wished three other people had been there. Two were, of course, Mr. Monogue and my grandmother, both of whom had passed away.

The third had died during my sophomore year of college. I won't share his name — but I'd like to share his story.

Rewind to my sophomore year of high school. A homeless guy usually stood outside our football practices. Mr. Charlie, who was like our team dad, would go to Publix and ask for the Danishes and muffins that were going to be thrown out at the end of the day. He then brought them to the field as after-practice snacks. We'd take home whatever was left over.

Whenever Mr. Charlie did that for us, I could not keep my eyes off that homeless man. We were stuffing our faces while he starved. One day, I grabbed a few muffins and asked him, "Hey, man, do you want these?" He shyly thanked me.

From then on, whenever Mr. Charlie brought us food, I made sure to save some for that man.

Then one day, the homeless man stopped me and asked, "Hey, can I talk to you for a second?"

"Yeah, sure, what's going on?" I asked.

He said, "I want to tell you something, and I hope you receive it."

"Alright," I said, a bit confused.

"God is going to use you in a very important way for years to come," he said.

I thought he meant I was destined for the NFL and appreciated the vote of confidence.

As time went on, I had regular conversations with him. One day, I asked a question that had been on my mind for some time. "Sir, how did you end up in this situation?" I asked.

"If I told you that I was CEO of a Fortune 500 company with a big house and a beautiful family, would you believe me?"

I said, "Well, if that's what you say, that's what I'll believe."

He said, "That's exactly what happened. Drugs, alcohol, and gambling completely tore my life up and tore me away from my family. I lost everything, including my daughter and son. They're five and seven, and I haven't seen them in three years. They're in Jacksonville with their mom, and she doesn't want to let them see me like this."

He then lamented, "I just want to get an opportunity to start making some money so that I can finally get myself back on track."

My teammate Todd Frier's father, Wayne, owned one of the largest mobile home distributor companies in the southeast. I asked Todd, "Do you think there is a chance that your dad could help this guy out?"

He said, "I don't know that man, but I'll trust you if you say he is a good man. I'll talk to my dad."

Mr. Frier hired him to clean up and serve as security at a new mobile home lot he'd opened. He even gave the man a mobile home to live in on that lot. I then learned that one of my coaches was good friends with this now formerly homeless man's ex-wife. They'd grown up together. So I asked that coach if he would invite her to our end of the season banquet. I didn't tell my coach my intentions. I did not want to divulge my real reason and risk her not coming.

I invited the formerly homeless man to the banquet and similarly kept him in the dark. I had no idea how things would turn out, but I figured that if there was even a small chance for a happy ending, then it was worth the shot.

When they saw one another, they both burst out crying and hugged.

She was there with her new husband, who told her former husband, "My wife and I pray for you every night. She never wanted to take your kids from you, but you were not in a place where you could be a dad. We've been praying that you get cleaned up and that you get into a better position so that you could be the father that you deserve to be."

It was a moment I can't even describe. They ended up reconnecting, and he again became a father to his kids.

Over the next few years, he continued to get promoted until he was pretty much running the south division for Wayne Frier Mobile Homes. He was out of the free housing, built a nice home, and remarried. He had a step-kid plus his kids from his first marriage. Life was good for him.

He came to my high school graduation and, before I left for the University of Florida, I went to see him. I told him that I still remembered how he told me God had plans for me. "When I make it to the NFL, I'm going to do the things you said God wants me to do," I said.

Like it was yesterday, I remember him looking at me and saying, "Whether you play in the NFL or not, that is not what I mean when I tell you God has great things in store for you. He's going to use you in many ways; football is not in the equation. You don't need to hold a football to serve God, and you have proven that through what you have done for me."

CHAPTER 11

This is not a wrestling book. If you were hoping that at some point I'd fill these pages with salacious stories about what goes on in the WWE locker room, personal real-life rivalries between wrestlers, and beefs I've had with my co-workers, I'm sorry to have disappointed you. But I'd be remiss if I didn't at least touch on my wrestling career.

Growing up, I was a WWE fan but never envisioned becoming a WWE Superstar. Looking back, though, maybe it was obvious that I'd become one.

To be a WWE Superstar, you need to be athletic, animated, and comfortable being nearly naked on television week in and week out. My fraternity used my apartment complex to throw pool parties that drew hundreds of attendees. I'd tell everyone in advance that they needed to come dressed to swim, not like they were going to a club. If a guy showed up over-dressed, I would playfully spear him into the water like I was WWE Hall of Famers Goldberg or Edge.

There is no doubt that I have always had what it takes to be a professional wrestler, but my journey to WWE was not a straight line. Yet, considering the platform that WWE has afforded me and the count-less children and adults that I've been able to help, I believe this was one of the greater parts of God's plan for me all along.

While I played a significant role in our football program at the University of Florida, I was not drafted by an NFL team. Yet, in the days immedi-ately following the draft, the Jacksonville Jaguars, Buffalo Bills, and San Francisco 49ers each invited me to their training camps. I chose Jacksonville so that I could remain in Florida.

I was confident that I could make the team and earn significant playing time. I played well, and my self-assurance swelled during the first few weeks of preseason. Then, during a routine pass rush drill, my right foot planted wrong and I heard a pop. It wasn't the most painful injury I'd ever endured, but I imme-diately knew that something was wrong. The MRIs confirmed that I'd torn my right ACL. My season was over, and my NFL career likely was too.

I was in a dark place for a while. Like many who had been in that position before me, I wondered,

"Is this ever going to stop? Why does it seem like I always have to overcome something?" I looked to God for answers.

I spent the next year rehabbing my knee. I took a job as defensive coordinator for my youngest brother's team at North Broward Preparatory School. During that time, I had second thoughts about pursuing a career as a professional football player: Maybe the injury was a sign that I needed to do something else. Maybe I could have a bigger impact as a coach rather than as a player.

It was while coaching that I realized that there is more to that job than Xs and Os. I also had to be a mentor, a counselor, a fundraiser, and even a parent to some. But my life experiences prepared me for those roles, and it felt like that was the career for me.

Then, while on a flight from Miami to Jacksonville to have my knee evaluated, I was seated next to Jim Ferraro, who owned the Las Vegas Gladiators in the Arena Football League. Due to my size, he of course asked if I was a football player. I told him about the injury and that my passion for playing the sport was dwindling. It was then that he offered me a job for his team whenever I was cleared to play.

I'd honestly never heard of arena football, so I told him that I doubted I'd be interested. But he explained the pay was good and that there were stories of players who had made it to the NFL based on their arena football success.

Once I was healed, my agent tried to get an NFL team to give me a look, but I couldn't even get a tryout. I'd been out of the game for a year and had never played a single NFL snap. In the pecking order of unsigned players, I was near the bottom. I called Mr. Ferraro and took him up on his offer. I enjoyed my time in arena football. I spent the 2004 and 2005 seasons in Las Vegas, 2006 in Tampa, and 2007 in Utah. Then I saw the writing on the wall: teams started folding, the pay got worse, as did the insurance. I knew it was time to find a new career.

During my off-season in Tampa, I'd coached for high schools. So I returned to Tampa and was hired as defensive coordinator at Chamberlain High School. I hoped to parlay that into a high school head coaching job somewhere in Tampa, but that never panned out.

I began discussing returning to the University of Florida to work with the football program in some capacity. That seemed like the path I would take, until WWE became an option.

It is no secret that one of my closest friends is former WWE Superstar and World Champion and current Hollywood movie star Dave Bautista. We lived close to one another and worked out at the same gym, so we became friends long before I started my career with WWE. Dave is a brother to me and an uncle to my sons.

It was Dave, who was already an established figure with WWE, who first suggested I seek out a career with the promotion. But I still did not think it was for me. Then one day, I was in South Tampa to pick up a pair of dress shoes, and across the street from the shoe store was the Florida Championship Wrestling facility. Before NXT, it was FCW that trained the WWE Superstars of tomorrow.

I called Dave and asked if the building on Dale Mabry Highway was what he'd been pressing me to check out. It was, he said, so I decided to poke my head in the back door.

The first person I met was Norman Smiley, and he directed me to WWE Hall of Famer Dusty Rhodes. At that moment, I couldn't stop thinking about how excited my grandmother would have been to hear I had been standing next to her favorite WWE Superstar. Dusty invited me to that night's show and told me that when it was over, I needed to seek out FCW president Steve Keirn.

I took my sons, Titus and T.J., who were five and three years old. During the show, I asked Titus if he'd want to see his dad in that ring someday. Excitedly, he replied, "It'd be cool." Then I asked T.J. if he thought I could do it.

"I think you can do anything, Daddy," he said.

I was sold.

Those first few weeks of training at FCW were hard. I was nervous as they taught me the needed skills. My body ached just as bad as it had during preseason football. I learned how true it was that the outcomes may be predetermined but the physicality was 100 percent real.

Just months into my training, I was cast in the next season of *NXT*, which began in June 2010. *NXT* was different then. It wasn't a promotion for up-and-coming talent. Rather, it was a nationally televised competition with the winner receiving a WWE contract.

I was nowhere near ready for that type of exposure. The first time I competed with NXT was in Tampa, my hometown. I was excited but also nervous because I'd be on national television. Up first was not a match but rather a keg-carrying competition.

This was the first literal stumble of my career.

One by one, the *NXT* contestants had to run around the ring, carrying a keg. The fastest time won the challenge.

As I stepped up, I honored my fraternity with our trademark bark, picked up the keg, began my sprint, and, just steps in, tripped and fell. It was the original Titus World Slide. It was embarrassing, to say the least.

Then came the promo to describe what I was trying to do. That didn't go well either. I told the crowd that's one of the reasons why you shouldn't drink. I said that if you do drink, you should definitely not drink and drive. I closed the promo by saying, "I'm just trying to make it a win." It was a total brain fart so, to no one's surprise, I was the first person cut from the competition.

I went back to FCW for more training, and, in March 2011, I was cast for another season of *NXT*. Titled *Redemption*, it featured Superstar hopefuls who failed to win the first *NXT* season. It was supposed to run seven weeks. Instead, it went for 59 episodes and, technically, it's still going on. No one ever declared an ending or a winner. They just abandoned the contest altogether, and I was moved to *SmackDown* full time. (Every time we won a competition, we were awarded Redemption Points. I still have a significant number that I'm waiting to cash in.)

Speaking of redemption . . .

Let's rewind again, this time to 2006 when I relocated to Tampa to play arena football. It was then that I first began attending the nondenominational church Revealing Truth Ministries in Tampa. I was in a bad place. My life had no balance. I was no longer having as much fun playing arena football as I once did, and I was tired of being on the road and away from my sons so often. Knowing that I needed a post-football career, I was dabbling in all sorts of business opportunities — some worked, some did not.

One day, I was at a Revealing Truth Ministries service when Pastor Greg Powe made his way down the aisle and stopped in front of me. He suddenly proclaimed in front of the all the parishioners, "God is going to elevate you, but he can't elevate you until you get out of your own way." He then went back to his preaching without addressing me again during that service.

I stuck around after the service and talked to Pastor Powe for a long time. Early in that conversation, I realized he was unlike any man of God I'd ever met. He let me be me and did not judge. He let me get angry. He let me cuss and raise my voice. I moaned and felt sorry for myself. My career wasn't where I thought it would be by then, nor was my personal life. It always seemed that whenever I took one step forward, something happened that knocked me 10 steps back, I lamented.

He let me know that he knew where I was coming from, and he shared his testimony with me. He had once struggled and had been in a dark place. But he realized that God had a plan for him. I told Pastor Powe that I knew God had a plan for me too, but I was growing frustrated that I had not yet been able to carry it out.

So he repeated what he'd told me in church. Getting out of my own way meant that I had to stop seeking opportunities and open my eyes to those opportunities that I probably come into contact with every day. He reminded me that what I do for a living is not who I am for a living. Once I embraced that belief and separated the two, he said, I'd be on the path I wanted.

Pastor Powe also reminded me that I needed to surrender to and have faith in God and trust his will. Once I let God lead the way, if I center myself around my faith and what God has called upon me to do, I can accomplish it all.

It was a year later that I first got involved in one of the church's philanthropic holiday events. The event helped people in need celebrate Christmas by giving meals and presents to around 200 families. I donated money for meals, picked up presents for the children, and volunteered my time on the day of the giveaways. I did the same in 2008, 2009, and 2010.

In the months leading up to the 2011 event, Pastor Powe mentioned that he wished the event could be larger. Wouldn't it be great, he asked, if we rented a park and added games and entertainment and made a day out of the event instead of a pick-up-and-go giveaway. But something like that would be too expensive.

During service one week, he again told the congregation of his vision. It was early on in my WWE career, when I was on TV as part of *NXT Redemption*. Still, I was being paid well, so in reply to Pastor Powe's words, I shot my hand up in the air and yelled out, "Let's do it. Whatever it costs, I will help take care of it."

Pastor Powe asked me why I was willing to commit to that.

"I feel like God is speaking to me," I said. "He is telling me that this is more than a church event. This can uplift the entire community."

And that created the Tampa Bay area's celebrated winter holiday charitable event now known as the Joy of Giving. Pastor Powe wanted it to be more than an event for just our church, and I had a similar vision. We wanted to invite other churches and community partners that did their own gift and meal giveaways and unite all those entities to give back to their community. We envisioned thousands of kids feeling the way I did when I received that remote-controlled car.

We rented a park and bouncy castles. Through church collections and numerous other donations, we were able to hand out nearly 500 gifts plus feed everyone in attendance. Just as we imagined, being out in the park rather than confined to our church grounds drew attention to the event. Other churches and community leaders asked to join the cause the following year, which gave me the idea to start recruiting others on my own.

It was around that time that my celebrity status was growing. I'd be out in public and fans would raise their arms in the sign of my fraternity and salute me with the Omega Psi Phi bark, perfectly mimicking how I entered the ring. I know not all the fans knew that was my shout-out to my historic Black fraternity. I'd bet none of my fans overseas did, yet they mimicked it anyway. That is the power of celebrity, and with that power, you can make a big difference.

As I've written numerous times throughout this book: being a television star helps. Yes, Thaddeus Bullard can ask for a meeting with the CEO of a major company and have some success. But when WWE Superstar Titus O'Neil asks for those same meetings, the success rate is much higher.

But I didn't just use my WWE celebrity status. In garnering support for this effort, I also reached out to people dating back to my days at the Boys Ranch, in Live Oak, the University of Florida, and those to whom I'd grown close while playing in the Arena Football League. WWE fans knew me because of my on-air personality. Those others knew me as someone with a big heart and a track record for successfully championing the underdog.

In 2016, the Joy of Giving gave out over 1,100 presents, more than double the inaugural year's total. As more local entities came on board and the event grew, those CEOs and community partners who only knew me from WWE were not just willing to meet with me, they were also inspired to be a part of what I was doing. I'd developed a winning track record, and they trusted that their money and time would be spent wisely.

So, in 2017, I decided to see how far we could push it. I wanted the Joy of Giving to be held at

Raymond James Stadium, and I wanted to hand out over 10,000 gifts.

People thought I was crazy. One of my partners of the event was Rob Elder, the same man who lives next door to Alec Barklage, the boy who defeated cancer in 2019. It was through Joy of Giving that we initially met. Rob is also president of Elder Automotive whose Replay Tampa Bay non-profit collects used sporting goods and redistributes the equipment to kids in need. Our first meeting was in August 2017, just weeks after I decided to go big-time with the event.

"So you're looking to do this in 2018?"

"No. Christmas season 2017," I said.

He stared at me blankly and asked, "What do you mean? That's in just a few months. That's impossible."

"Nothing is impossible," I said. "We'll get it done."

Elder later admitted he told others, "There is no way he is going to pull this off. I've done a lot of parties and events in my lifetime for 1,000 people, and those took months and months of planning. He's going to pull one off for 10,000 kids in four months, plus do it at Raymond James? Give me a break."

He still agreed to do what he could to help. Two months later, during a meeting with all the community partners, I informed them that we'd already collected 7,000 gifts. It was at that moment that everyone in the room finally believed in me. With the help of community partners like PDQ, 4 Rivers Smokehouse, Dippin' Dots, Elder Automotive, DEX Imaging, and all of the local professional sports teams — the Rays, Lightning, Bucs, Rowdies, and Tarpons — we made it happen that year. We gave out 10,000 gifts — everything from Easy-Bake Ovens to bicycles to gaming systems to tablets. And we provided stage concerts, free food for all, and other forms of entertainment throughout.

Non-profits and government agencies that provide social services to the less fortunate also set up tables throughout the stadium so that those in attendance knew that the type of help that could transform their lives was available. To keep it organized, all attendees had to register online in advance. The last thing I wanted was for more kids to show up than we had presents for.

During that 2017 event, three siblings ran up to me, excited to meet WWE Superstar Titus O'Neil. Their mom had no idea who I was, but she was ecstatic to see her kids so happy. But then she broke my heart. She didn't know about the registration, nor could she have even signed up if she had known because she could not afford internet. Shielding her face from her kids, she broke down in tears and confided in me that she was trying so hard to be a good mom but felt like she just kept failing them. There would be no presents under the tree that year, she said, and she had no idea how to explain that to her kids.

I promised that her kids would have their best Christmas ever.

I handed her $300 in Walmart gift cards and told her to make sure the family had a Christmas feast to remember, plus food for the next few weeks. I walked her kids to the tents where the presents were kept. Every kid in attendance could take one present home. I told those kids that they could each take three.

The mom flung her arms around me and sobbed tears of joy. As I hugged her back, I didn't see a random woman I'd just met. I saw my mom. As her kids bounced from toy station to toy station in search of the perfect presents, I saw 12-year-old me being handed that remote-controlled car.

Among the others in attendance at the 2017 Joy of Giving event were kids from the Boys Ranch. I had something special planned for them. Besides each receiving a gift from the tent, I also bought each ranch cottage a gaming system and big screen TV. Wanting those to be a surprise, I called the ranch kids up on stage in front of the thousands who were in attendance and presented them with the cottage gifts. The kids jumped up and down, high-fived, and hugged. That was my full-circle moment.

That moment wasn't about the toys, though. It was about much more than that. I wanted them to look into the crowd and realize that all those kids were there because they too came from families who struggled. I wanted them to see that they were not alone. I wanted them to realize that I was once like them but am now in the position to pull off events of that magnitude. I wanted them to realize that anything is possible and that one day they too could be in the position to change someone's life.

Most importantly, I wanted them to know that I loved them and that I believed in them.

In writing this book, I've shared a lot about myself, all with the hope that you will understand that if you change a person's life at an early age, you never know who that person will become.

I once heard the phrase, "Uncoachable kids become unemployable adults." That's wrong. Just because a kid is not coachable does not mean that they are a bad kid and just because an adult is unemployed does not mean that they're a bad person. It just means that somewhere along the way, the environment wasn't right for that person to thrive. I hope that after reading this book, rather than automatically labeling a kid or an adult as troublesome, you take a deeper look at who they are and question why they might be acting out and think of how you can help them.

Various countries like to say that they're the greatest nation in the world, but no country can be great until its citizens learn to be the greatest people in the world. The way that you do that is to move past stereotypes, dive deeper into a culture, dive deeper into a situation, and dive deeper into an environment so that you can truly understand what others may or may not have gone through.

Hopefully, you now understand why I came to the decision and the understanding that there is no such thing as a bad kid. There are kids who are in bad situations and who are making bad decisions. When you take those "bad kids" and move them into a great environment around great people, they'll have a greater chance to succeed.

That is *my* story. I was a kid who people assumed would be dead or in jail by the time he was 16. But today I enjoy numerous accolades, achievements, and successes. I didn't achieve these things because I was the biggest, or the strongest, or the smartest. Rather, I succeeded because I had people willing to invest in me even when they gained nothing in return.

I try my best to live two rules.

Rule number one: Love and respect everyone with whom you come in contact. You may not agree with them, but you can love and respect them.

Rule number two: Do not use the word *can't*. From a biblical sense, my faith lies in God and Jesus and the word of God. In the word of God it says, "We can do all things through Christ who strengthens us." The Bible only uses the word "can't" when referencing sins. So if I'm professing that's my faith and that's where my faith lies, I should exercise that faith and realize that there is really nothing that I cannot do.

For most of my young adult life, people listed all the things I wouldn't be able to do, and it all proved to be a lie. I did graduate from high school, I did graduate from college, I did play professional football, and I did make something of myself against the notion that I wouldn't. But my greatest pride doesn't come from my own accomplishments, it comes in the form of seeing other people thrive and rise above the stereotypes and stigmas that challenge them.

And so, I challenge every adult to better themselves, for the youth around them and for the world they live in. Every day, we should all wake up and promise to be better for ourselves, be better for others, and be better for the world. I know that it can be difficult when you're dealing with things like bills, schoolwork, family, relationships, and every obstacle life throws at us. But as long as we all have blood and breath in our bodies, we have the opportunity to do better. We have a chance to make a significant impact both in our own lives and in the lives of others.

What will you do to ensure that the kid next door, the kid down the hall, the kid who's your friend, or even the kid who is your foe doesn't get repressed by the mantra of being a "bad kid"?

The day prior to the 2017 Joy of Giving event, I called my mom and asked if she realized that her decision to give birth to me has helped hundreds of thousands of people. Not just thousands, but hundreds of thousands. Because via social media, newspapers, the TV news, or direct contact, I've inspired so many others to give back to the community, who then inspired others who inspired others and so on.

I told my mom that the next day, I would be hosting an event at a football stadium that will bless thousands of families who come from the same situation that we came from, some worse. And they'll all leave with smiles on their faces. Some of them want a meal in their belly, and some want to escape their reality. I told her I think about the lives I have changed. I see kids who are graduating from college, parents who are buying their first home, kids who come from families where no one had ever graduated high school get accepted to schools like Cornell University, Florida State University, the University of Florida, Harvard University, and many more — and, to think, I had a hand in all this.

We both cried and thanked God for all he had done.

My beginning was not very good, but there was nothing I could do about that.

I can, however, determine my ending.

And it will be special.

No kids can dictate their beginnings. But, collectively, we can be the force that leads them to a special ending. We can all be a Patrick Monogue, who uttered the words, "I love you and I believe in you," which changed my life. We can all be the person who tells a child that "there's no such thing as a bad kid."

Today, I understand why Mr. Monogue wouldn't explain exactly what he meant. I understand now why he said I would figure it out on my own. I now know what he knew. The words spell it right out. There is no hidden meaning. There is no such thing as a bad kid means there is no such thing as a bad kid — period.

There are kids in bad situations; kids surrounded by bad influences; kids who make bad decisions. But take those same "bad kids" and put them in a good situation, surrounded by good people, and they will have a greater chance of success. That is the story of my life and the lives of countless others.

So the next time you see a kid acting out — yelling, cursing, or fighting — dig deeper, investigate the past, show them that you genuinely love and care for them . . . and above all else, be patient.

It is our job to make the world around us better in every way possible. Sometimes we can do it financially, other times spiritually, even verbally, or physically. However we do it, if it is done with love, respect, and truth, positive change is inevitable — the youth of today will be the positive leaders and changers of tomorrow.

There's no such thing as a bad kid.

There's no such thing as a bad kid.

There's no such thing as a bad kid.

Repeat those words, then go out each day and put what they mean into practice and into action, with love, honor, and dignity . . .

— Thaddeus "Titus O'Neil" Bullard,
the once-labeled "Bad Kid"

At ECW Press, we want you to enjoy this book in whatever format you like, whenever you like. Leave your print book at home and take the eBook to go! Purchase the print edition and receive the eBook free. Just send an email to ebook@ecwpress.com and include:

- the book title
- the name of the store where you purchased it
- your receipt number
- your preference of file type: PDF or ePub

A real person will respond to your email with your eBook attached. And thanks for supporting an independently owned Canadian publisher with your purchase!